Dedicated to all curious and creative children. May this coloring book bring joy and inspiration to your discovery journeys. With love, WILME.

WILME
2024

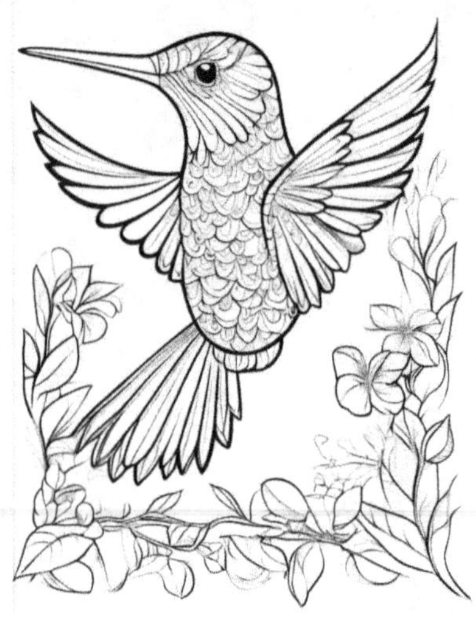

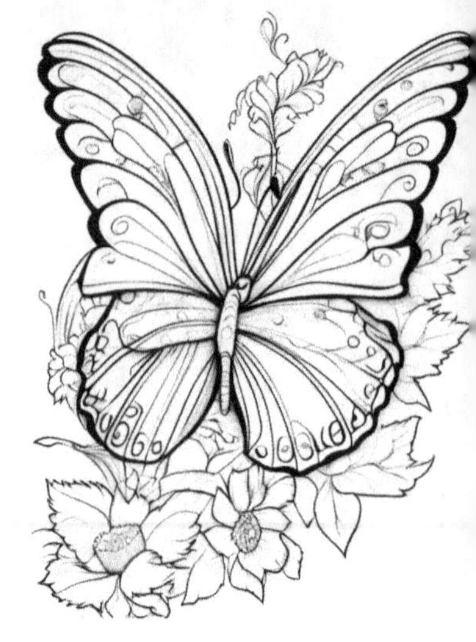

THIS BOOK BELONGS TO:

____

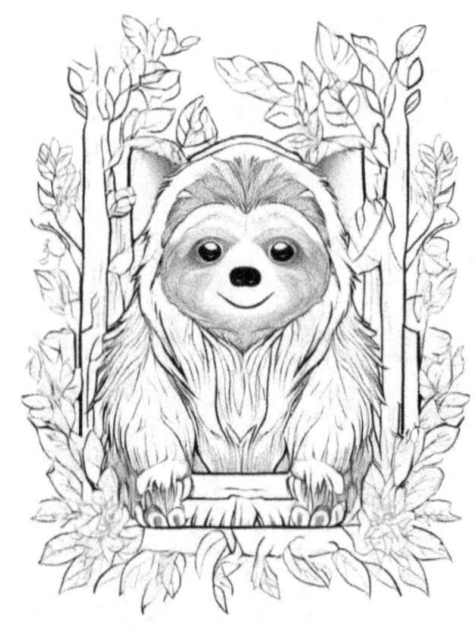

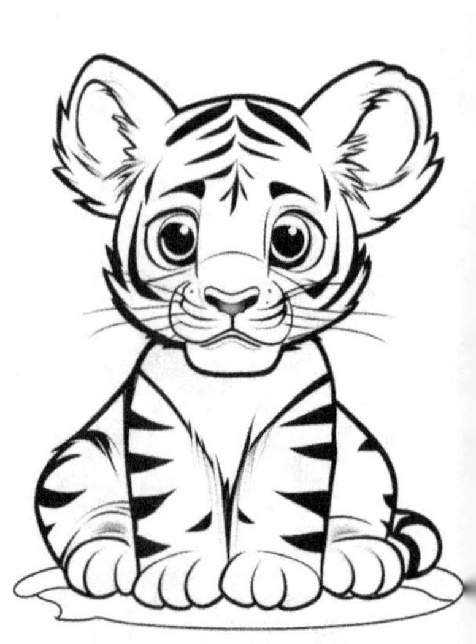

Test Color Page

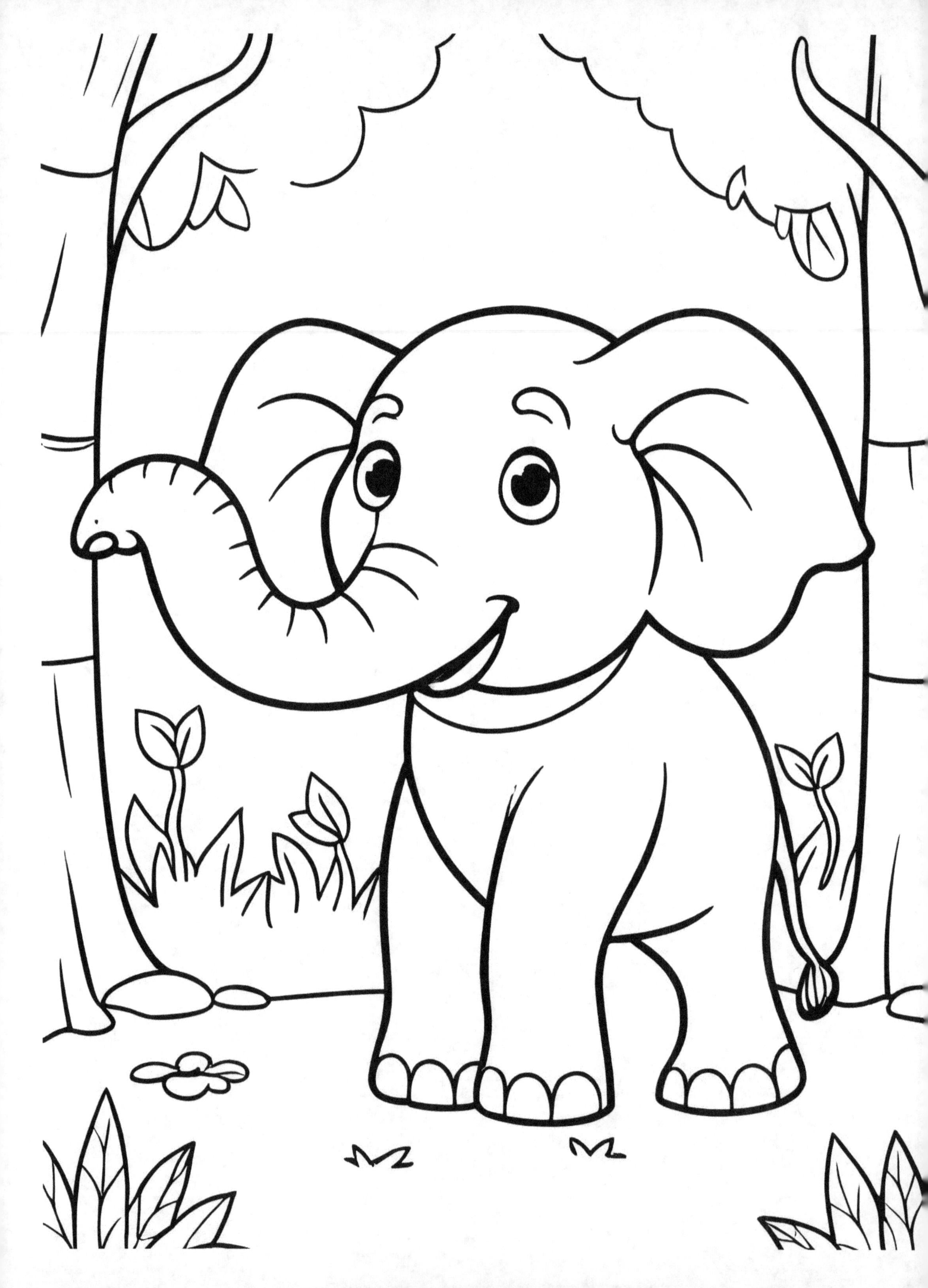

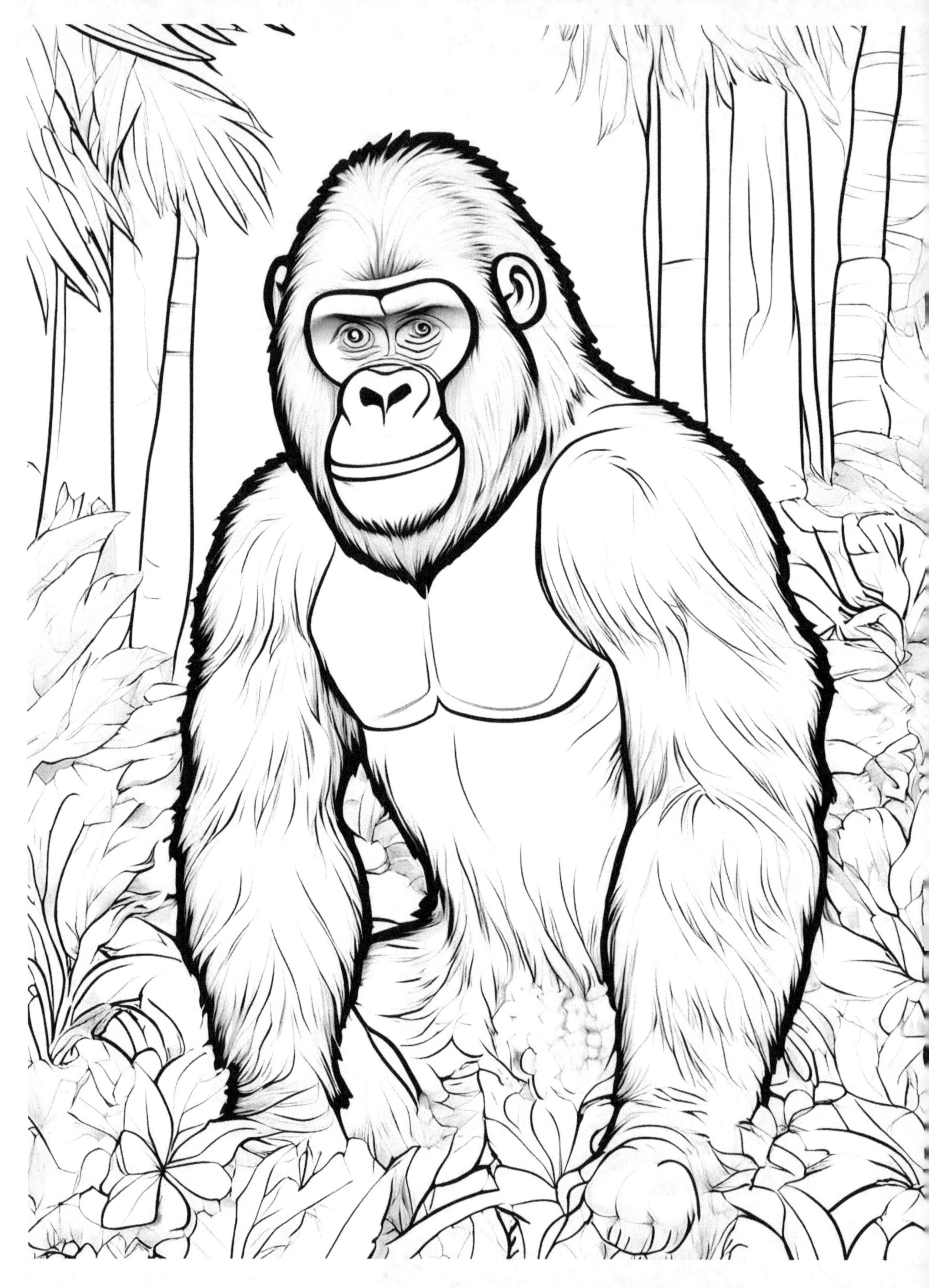

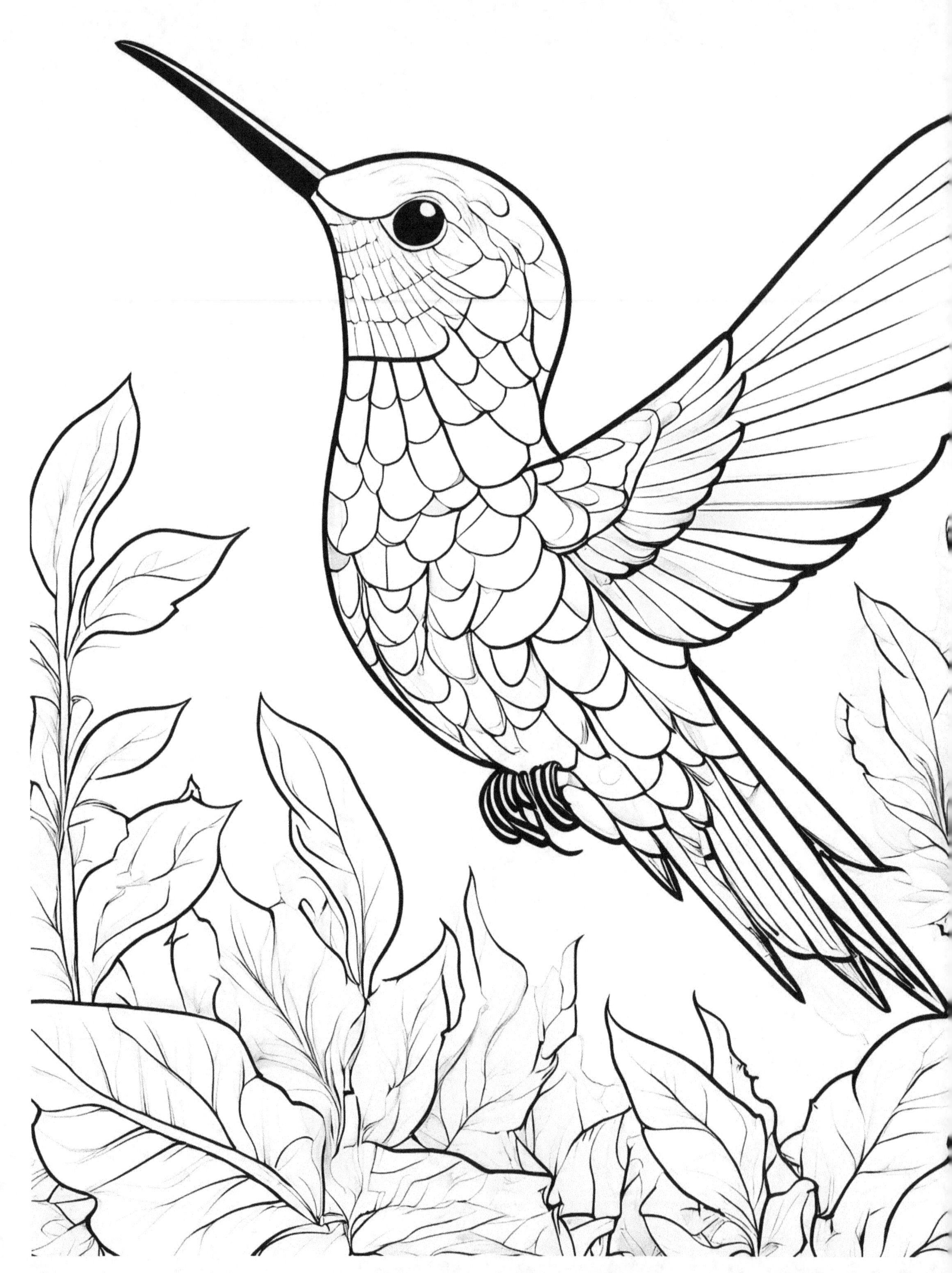

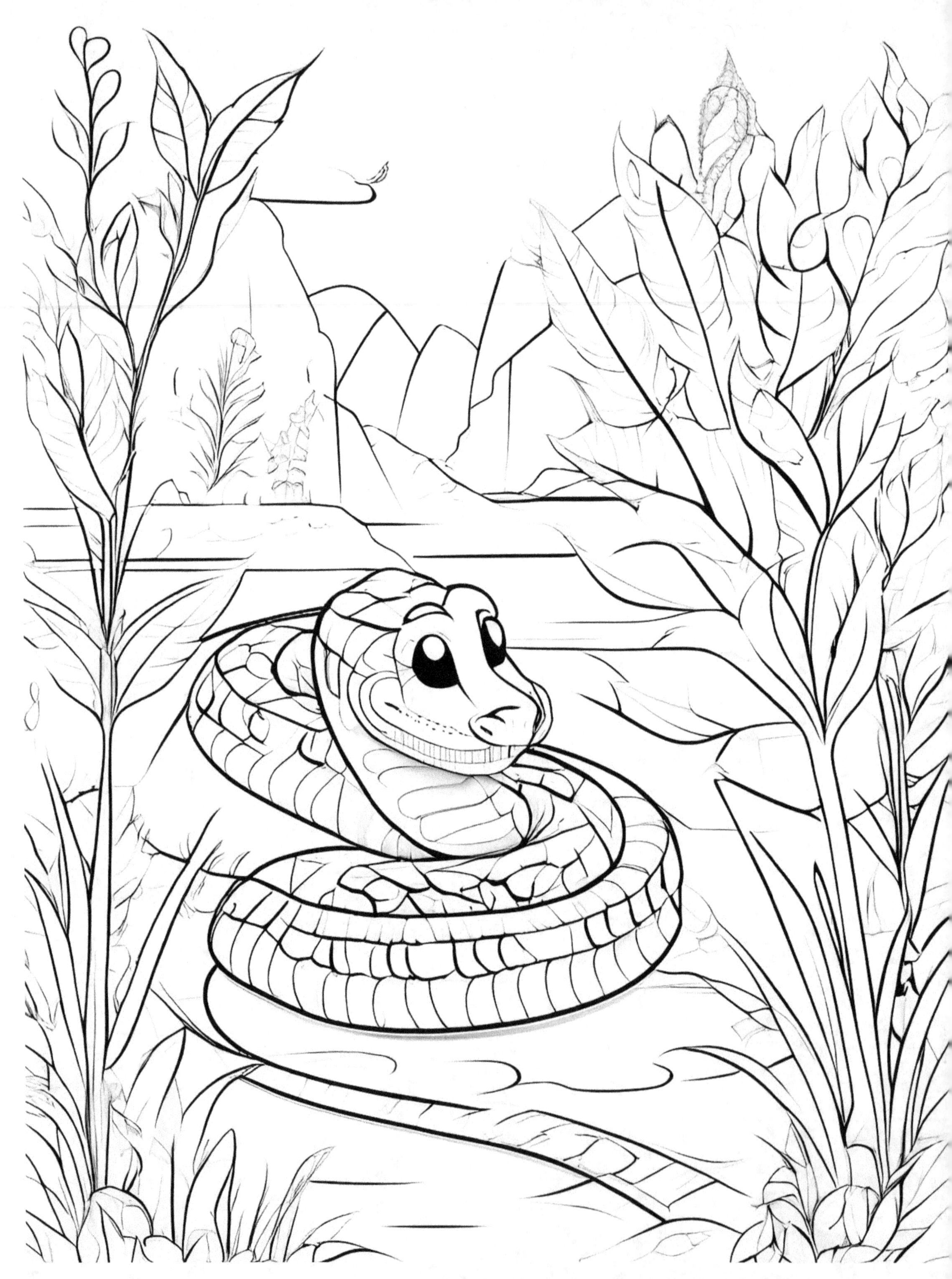

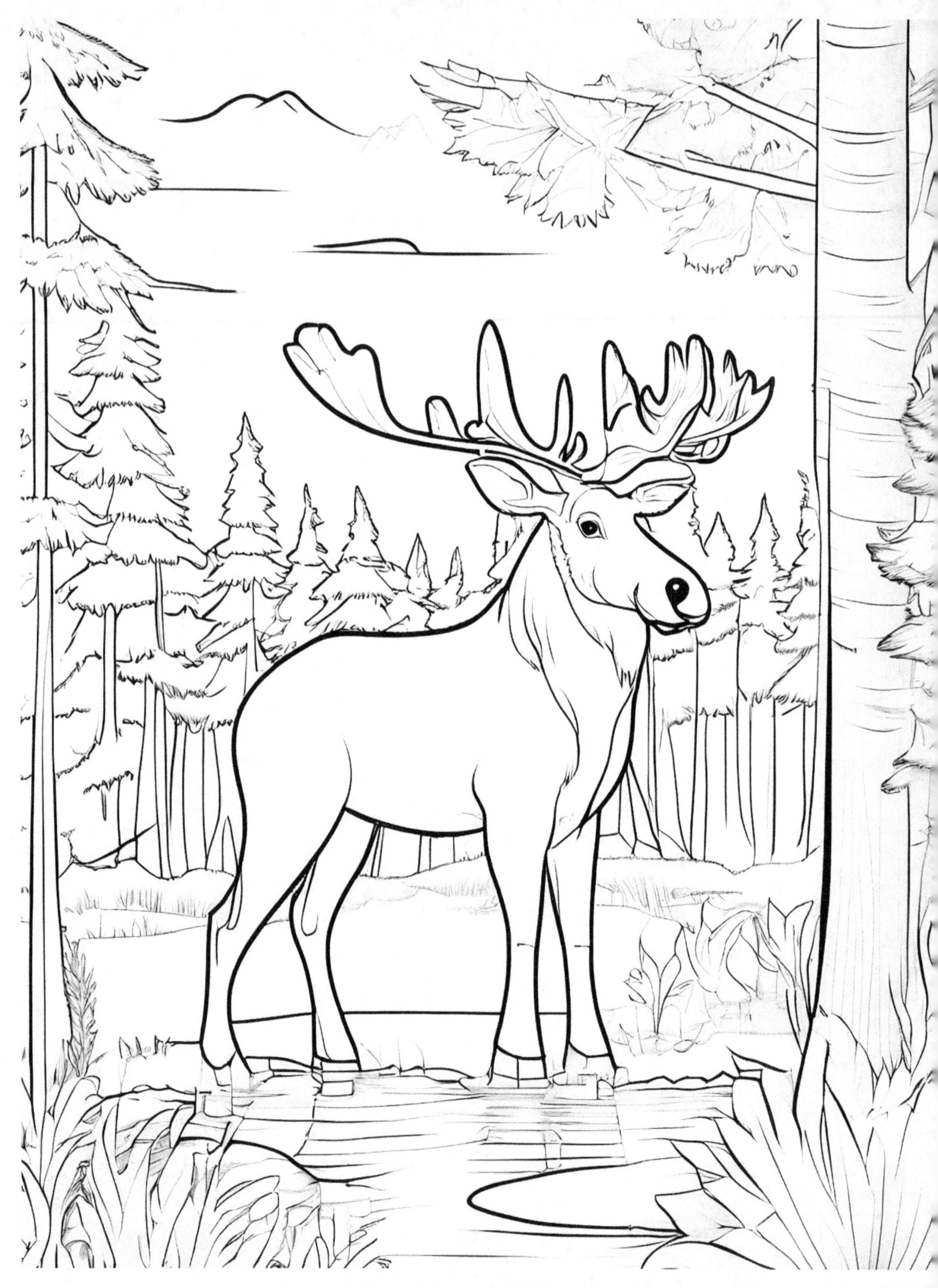

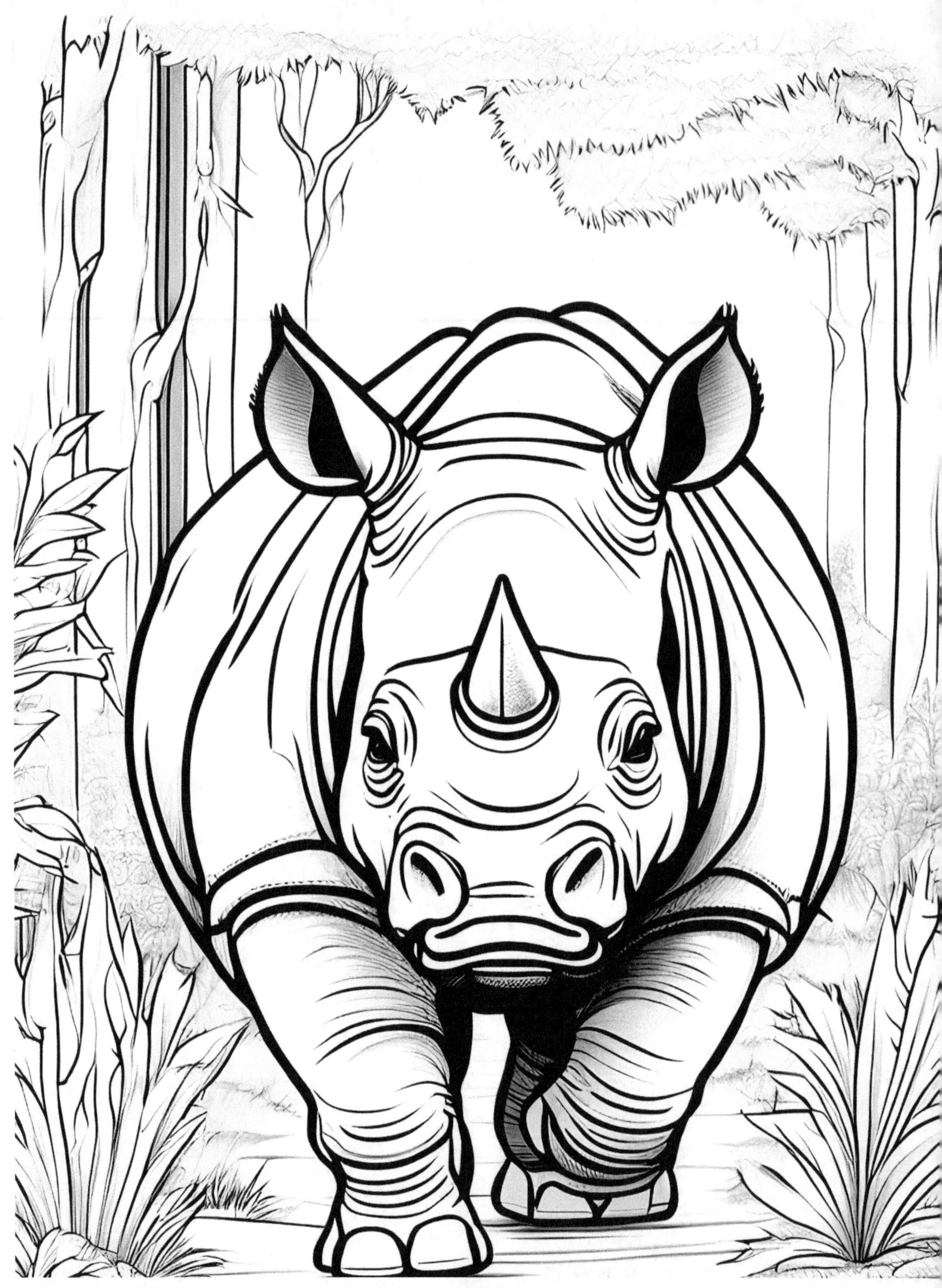

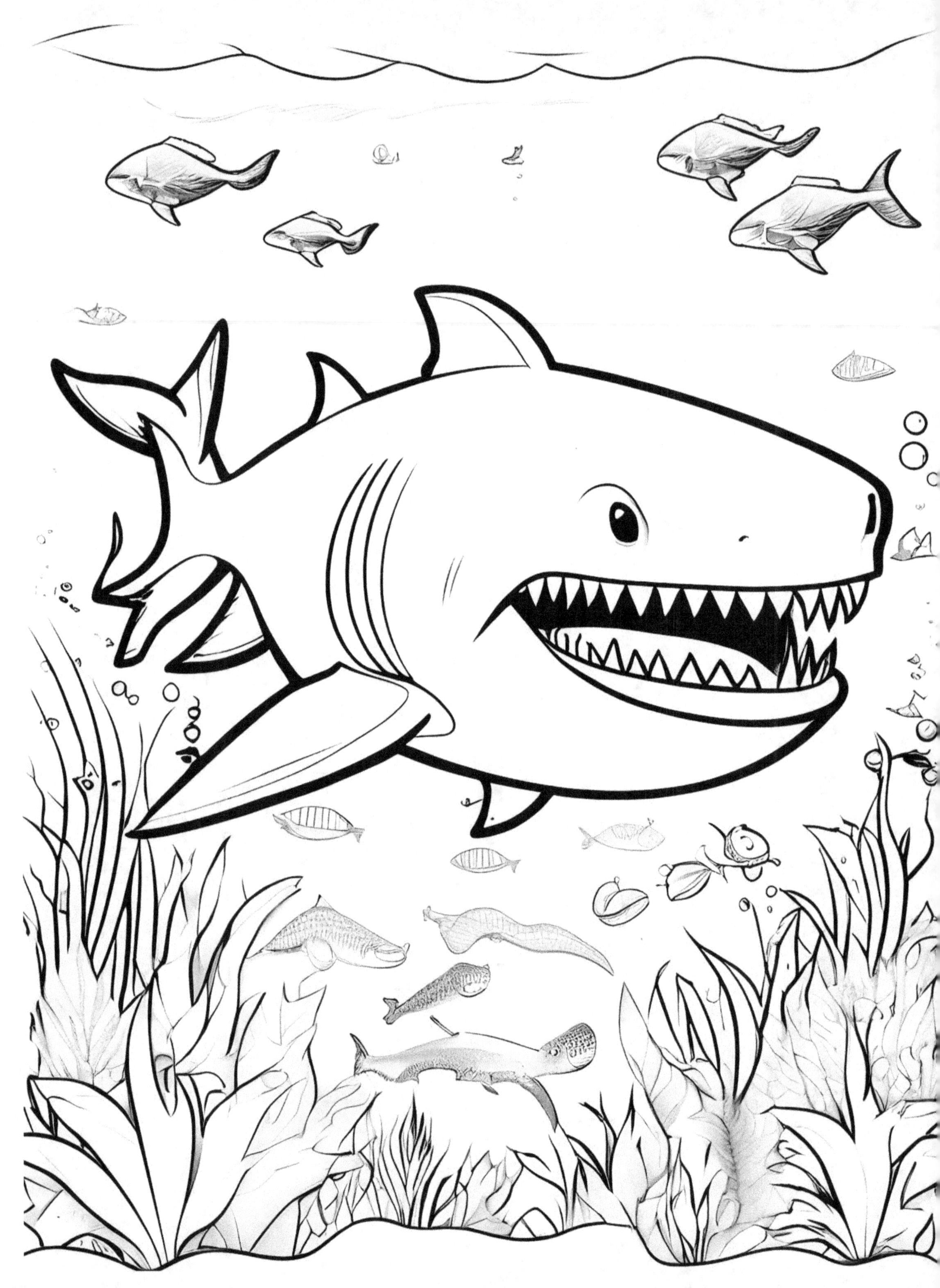

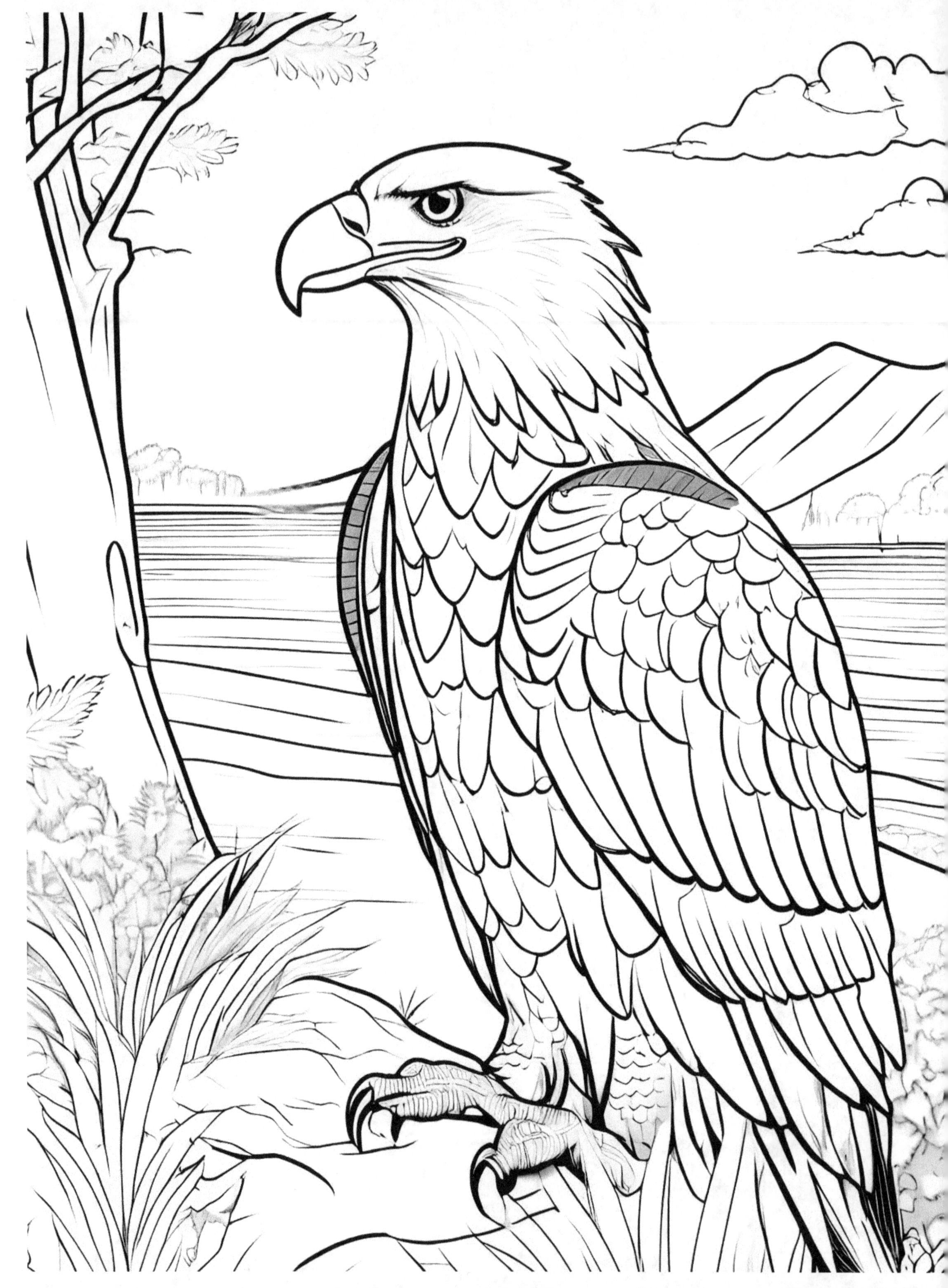

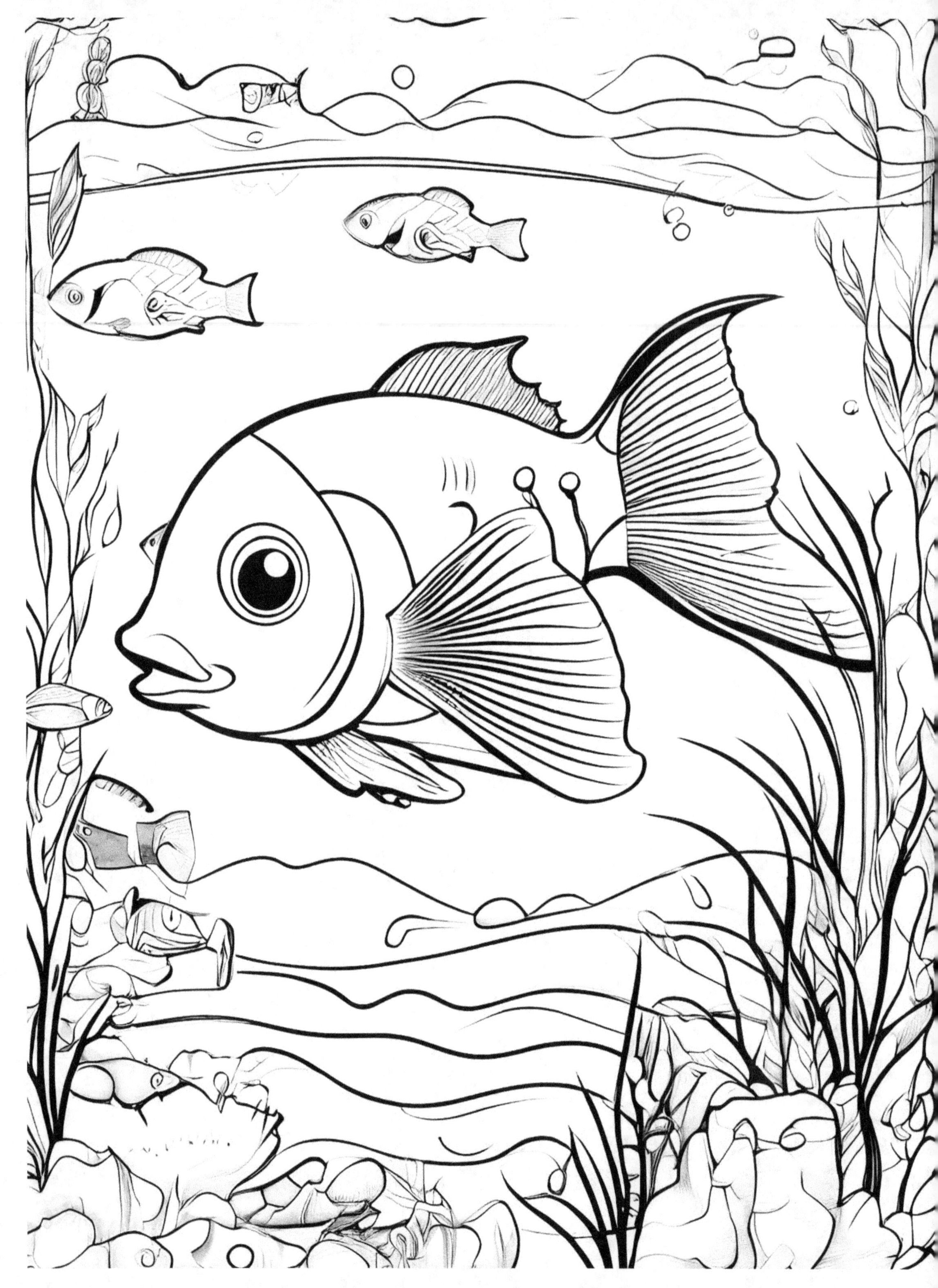

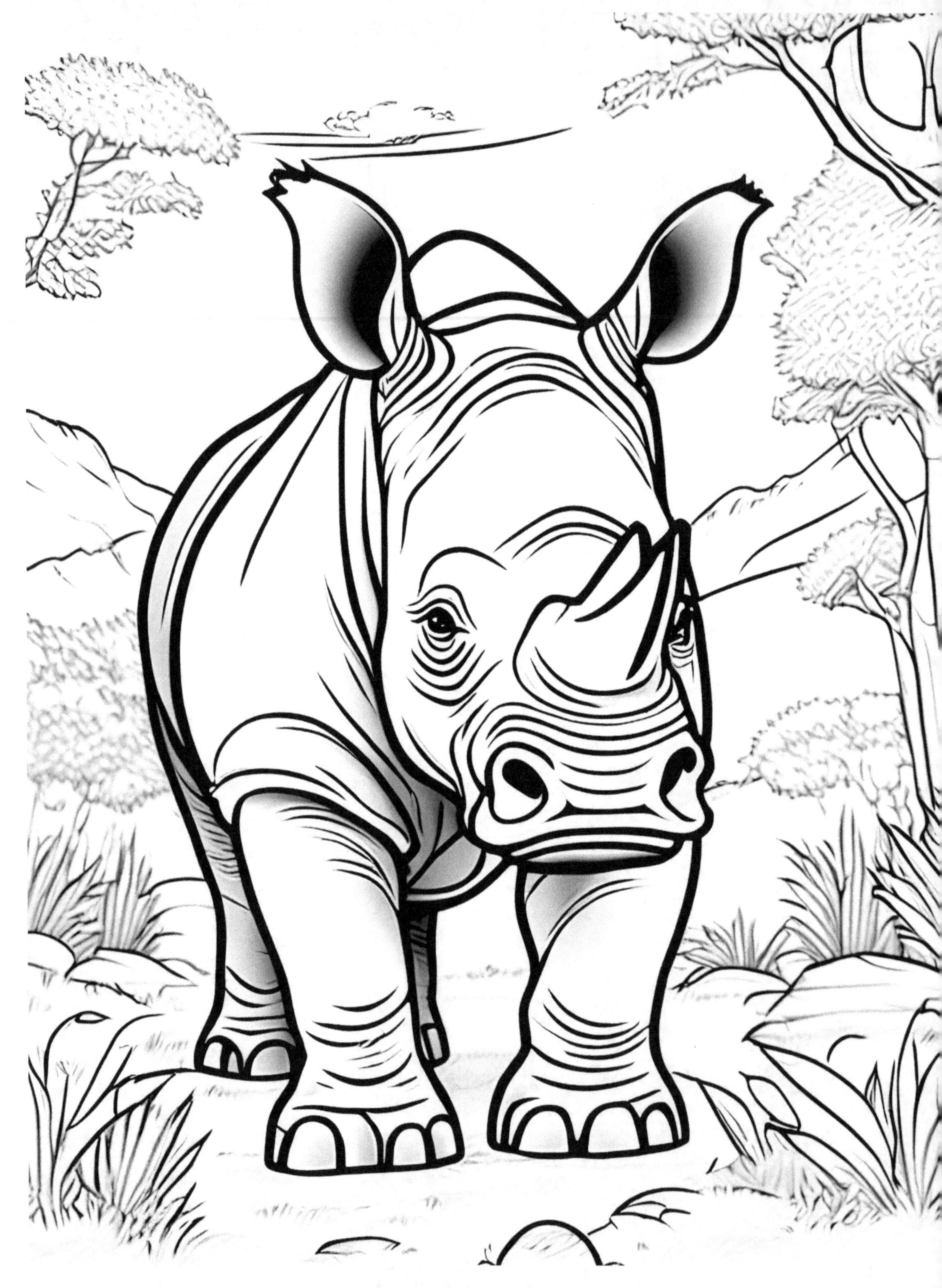

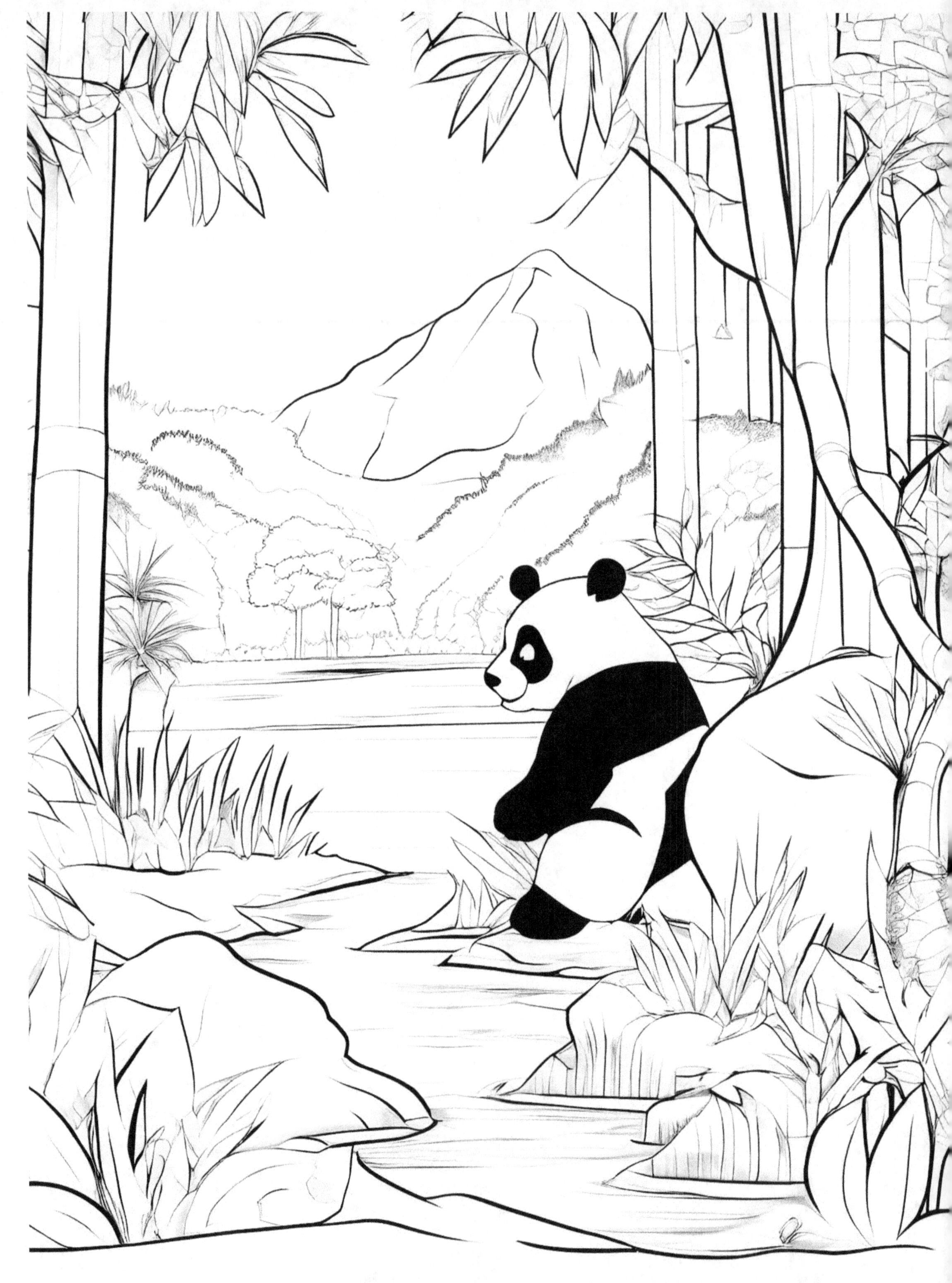

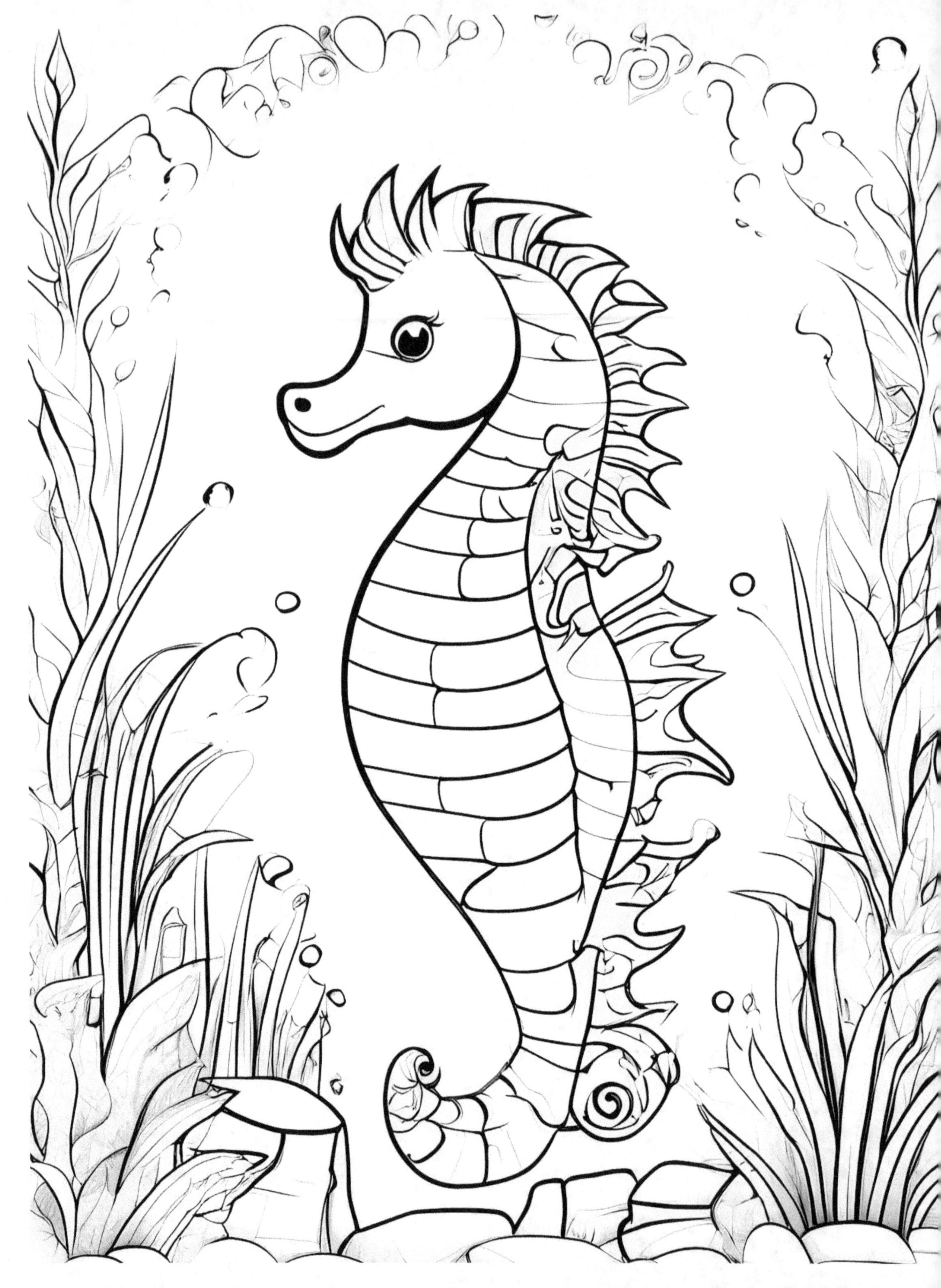

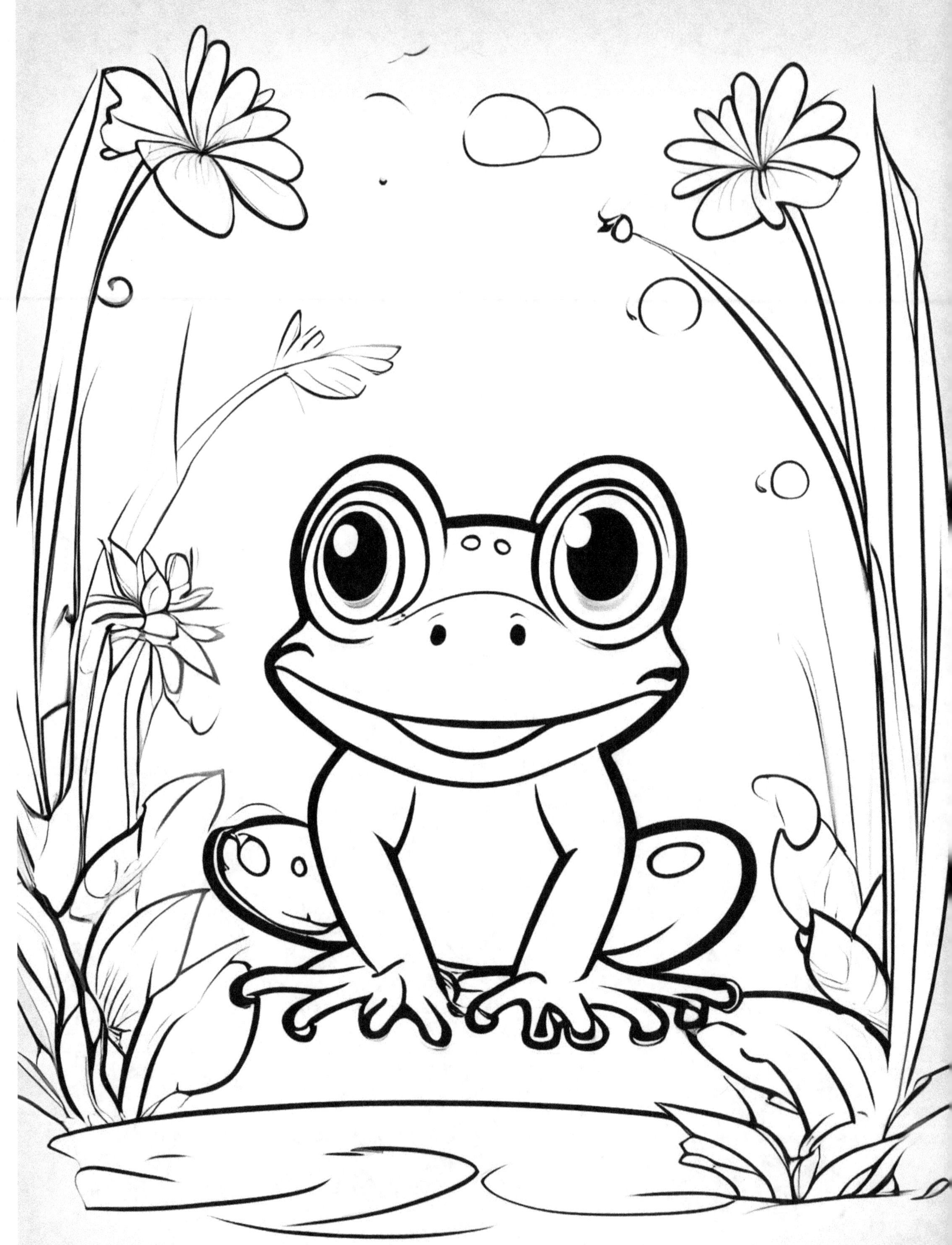

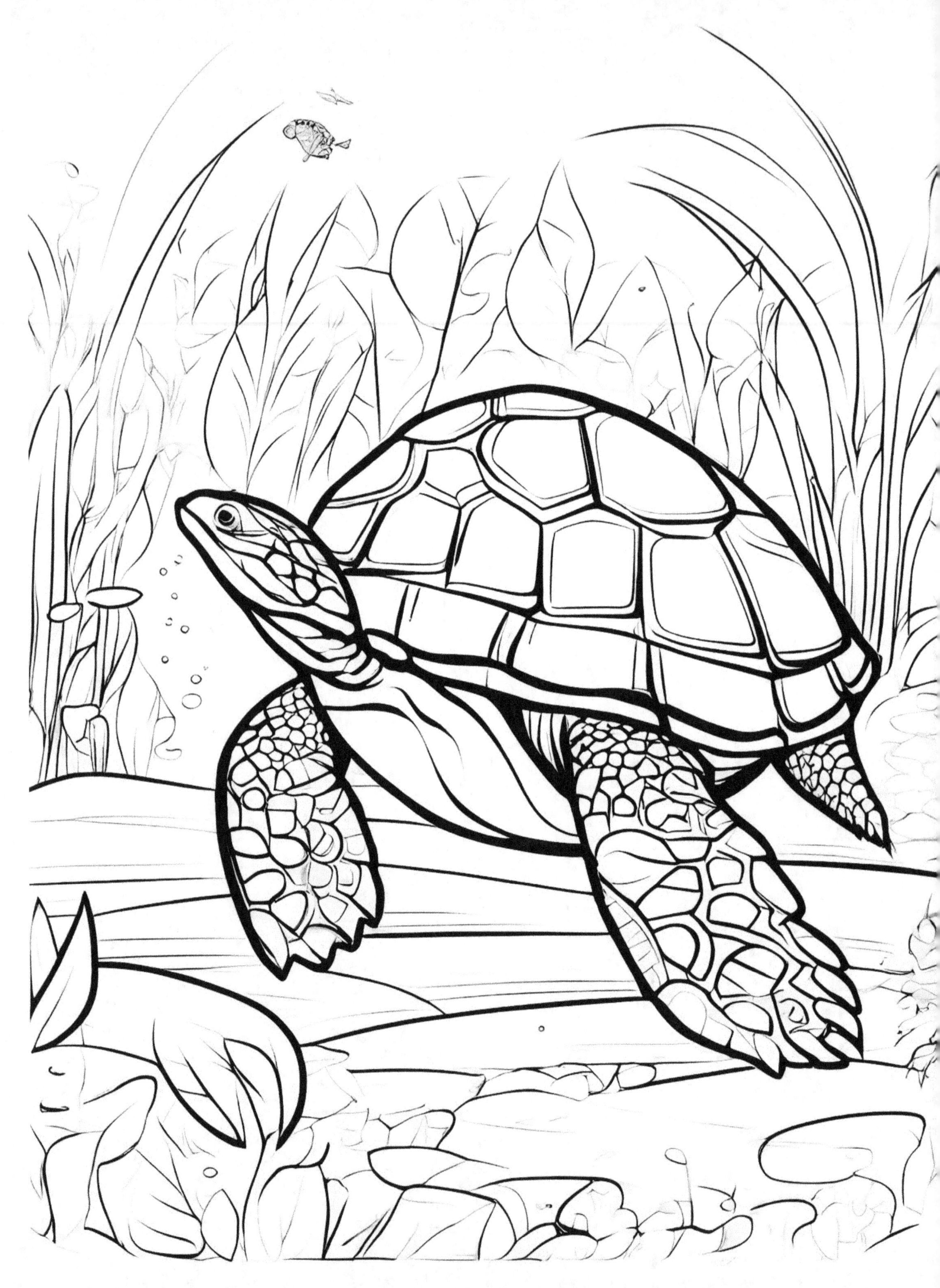

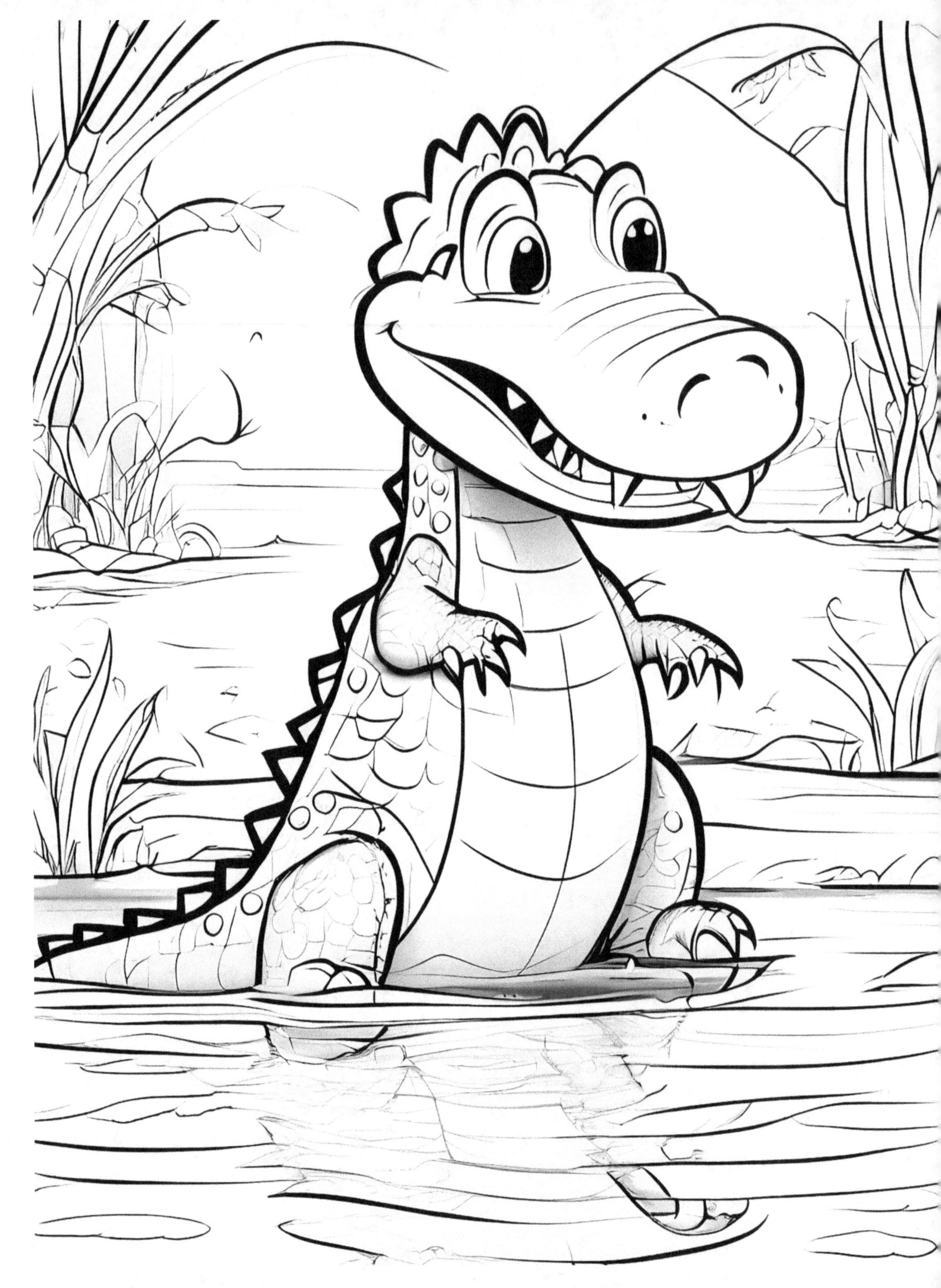

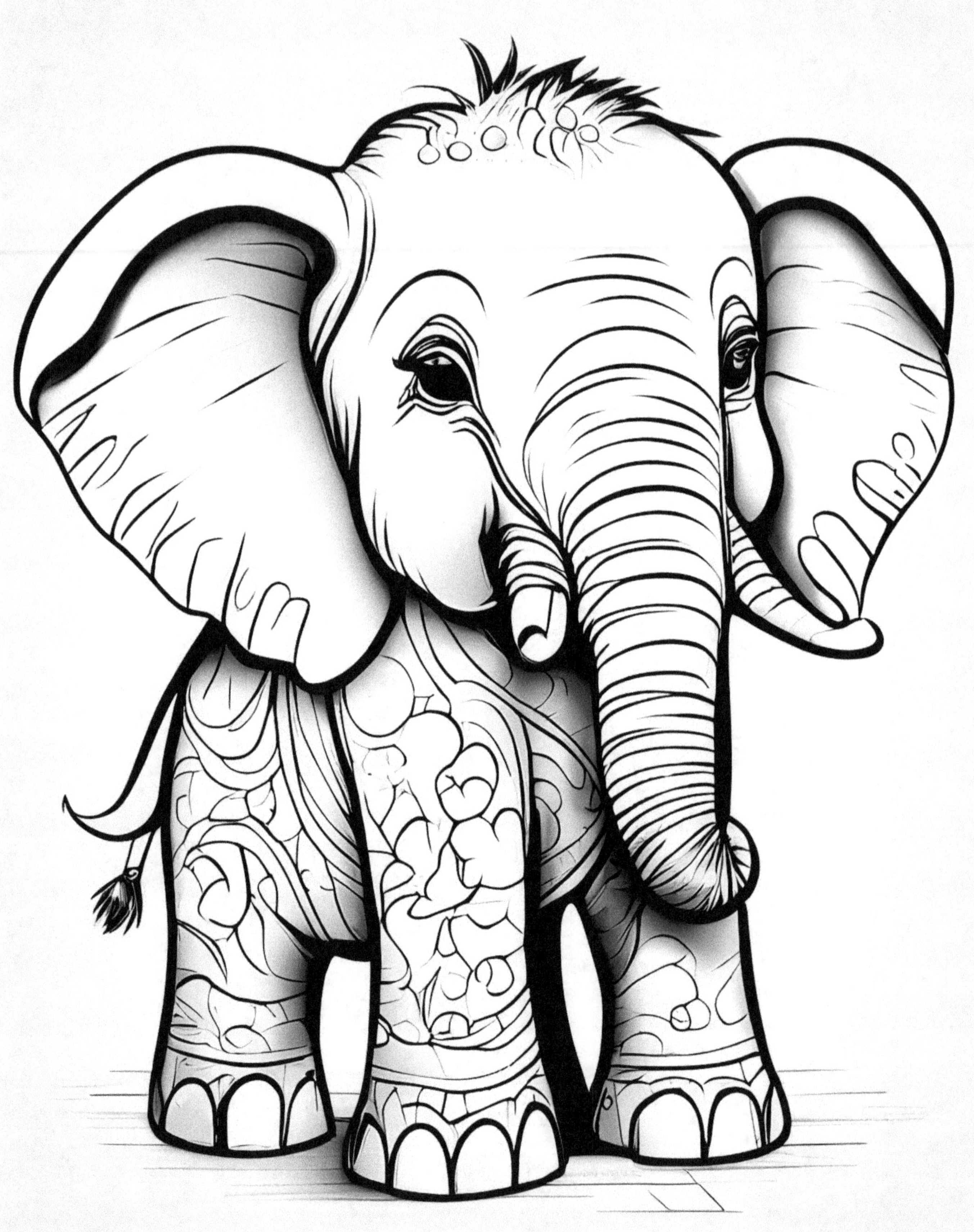

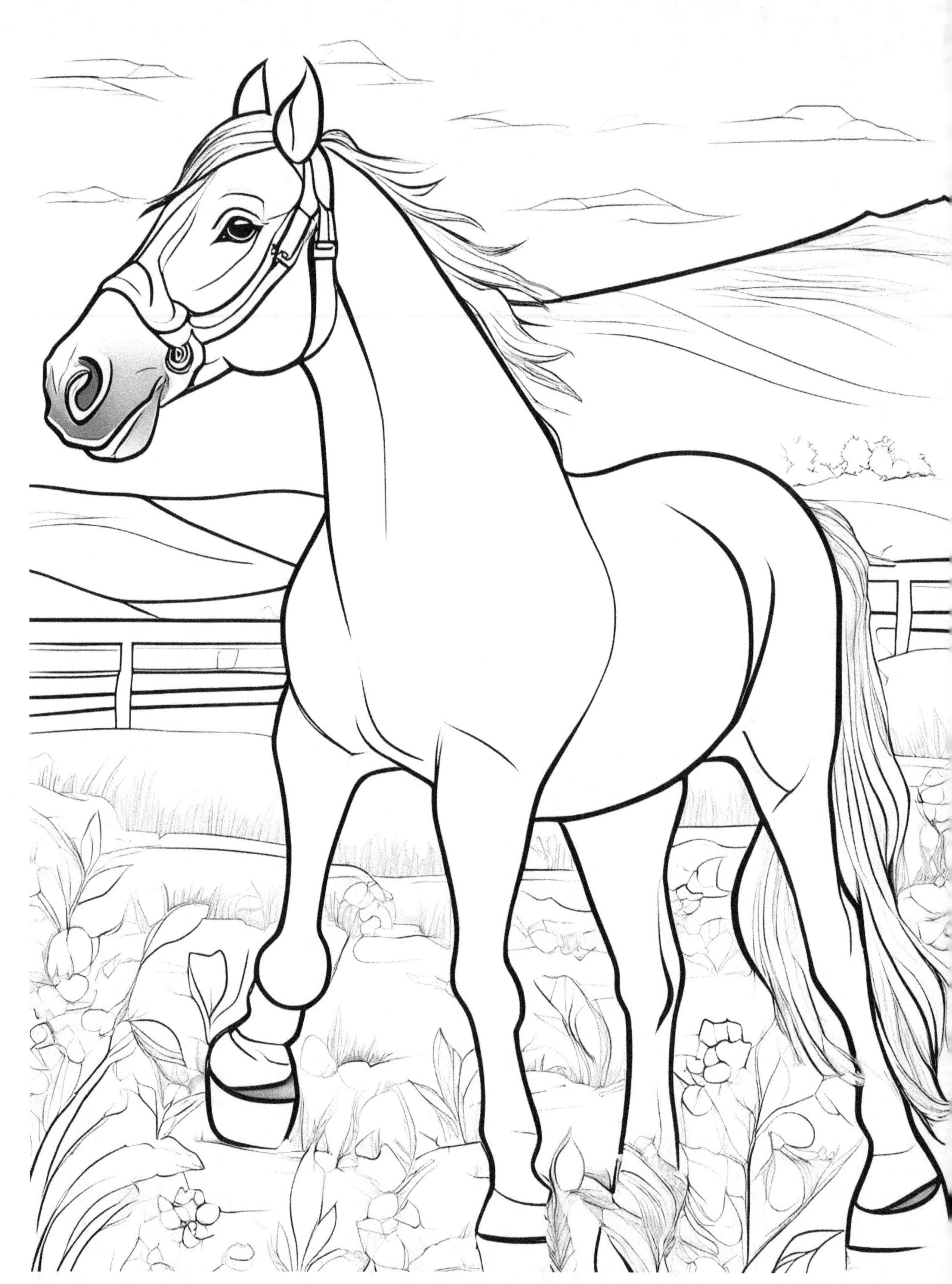

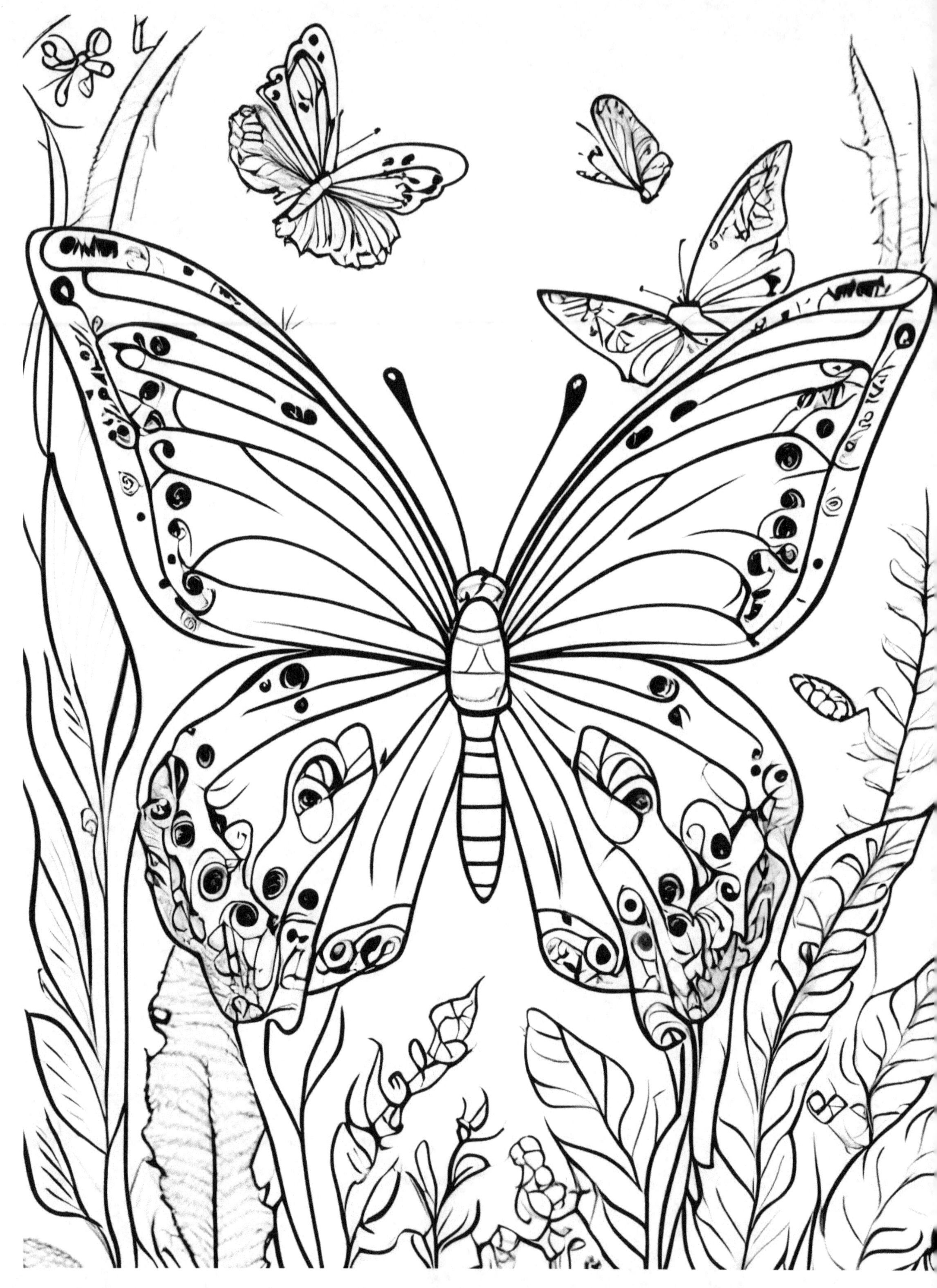

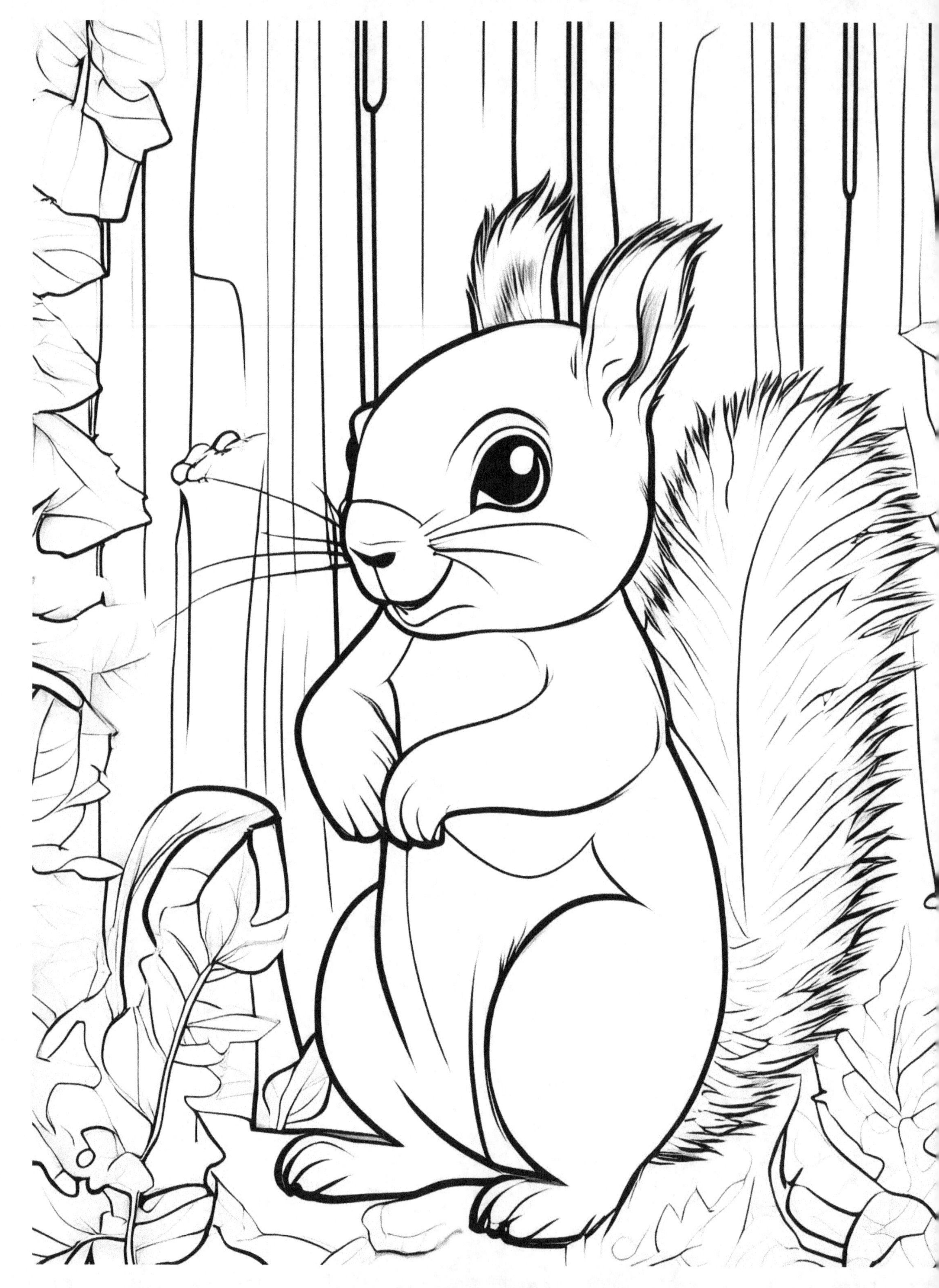

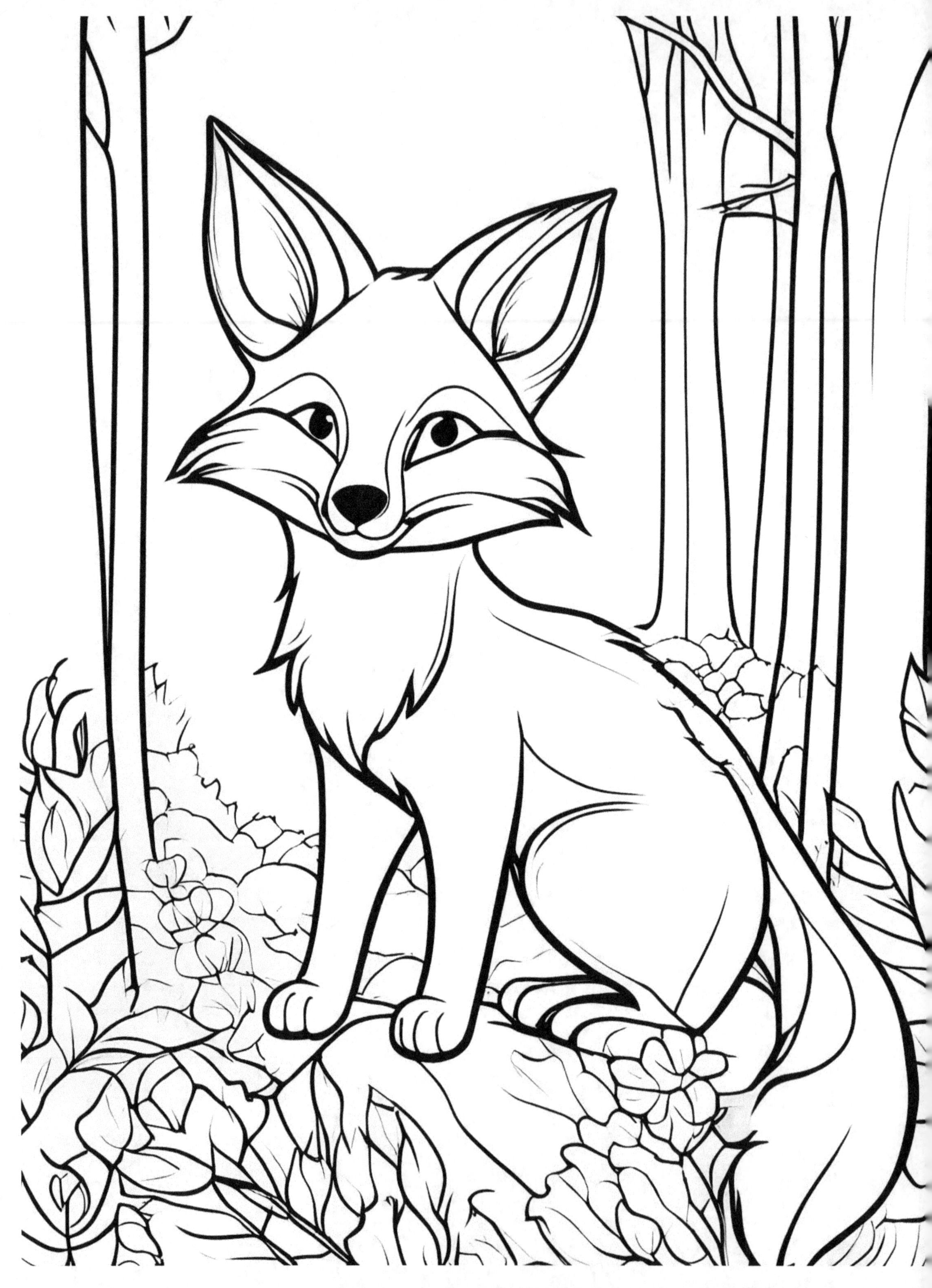

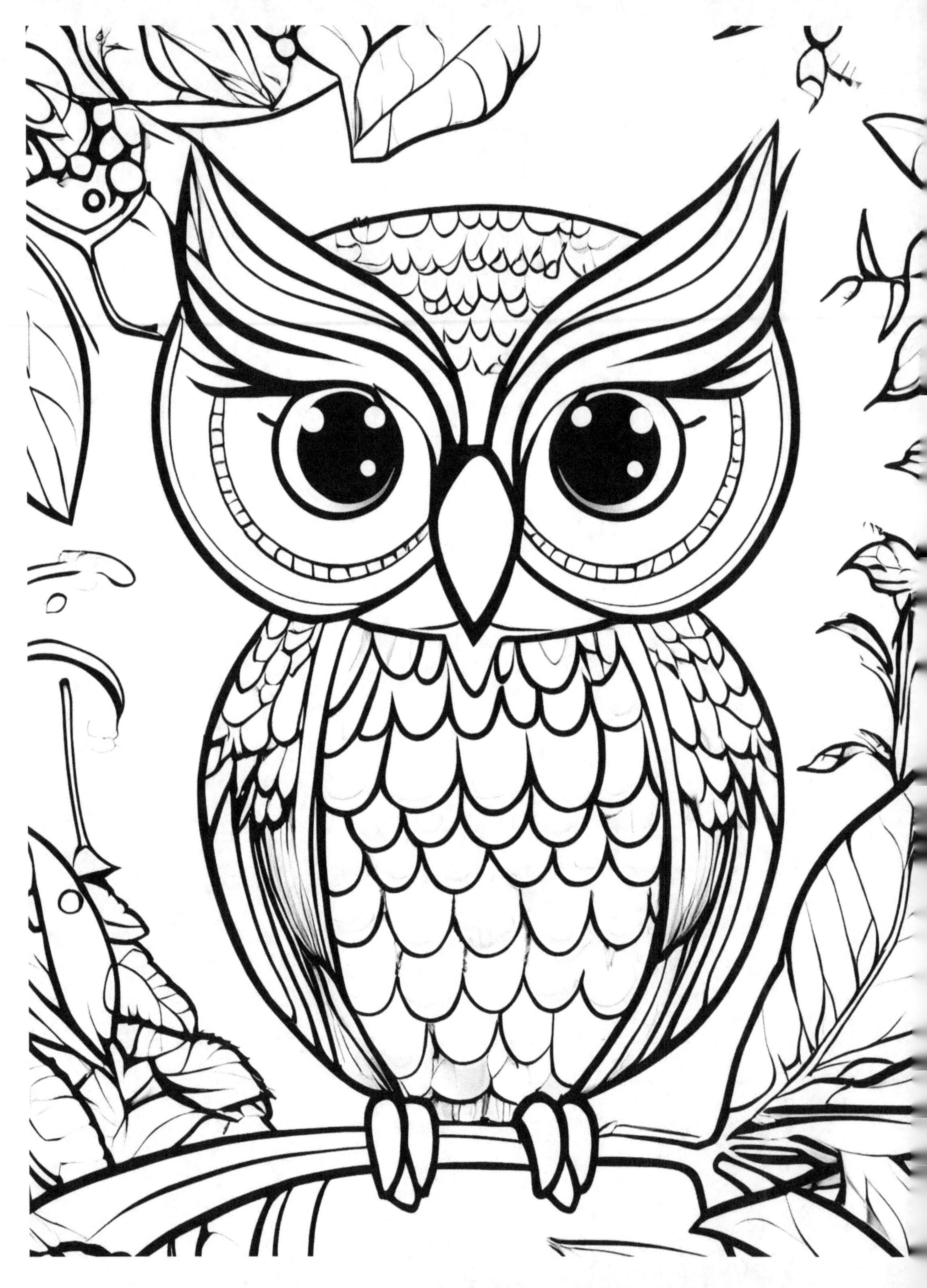

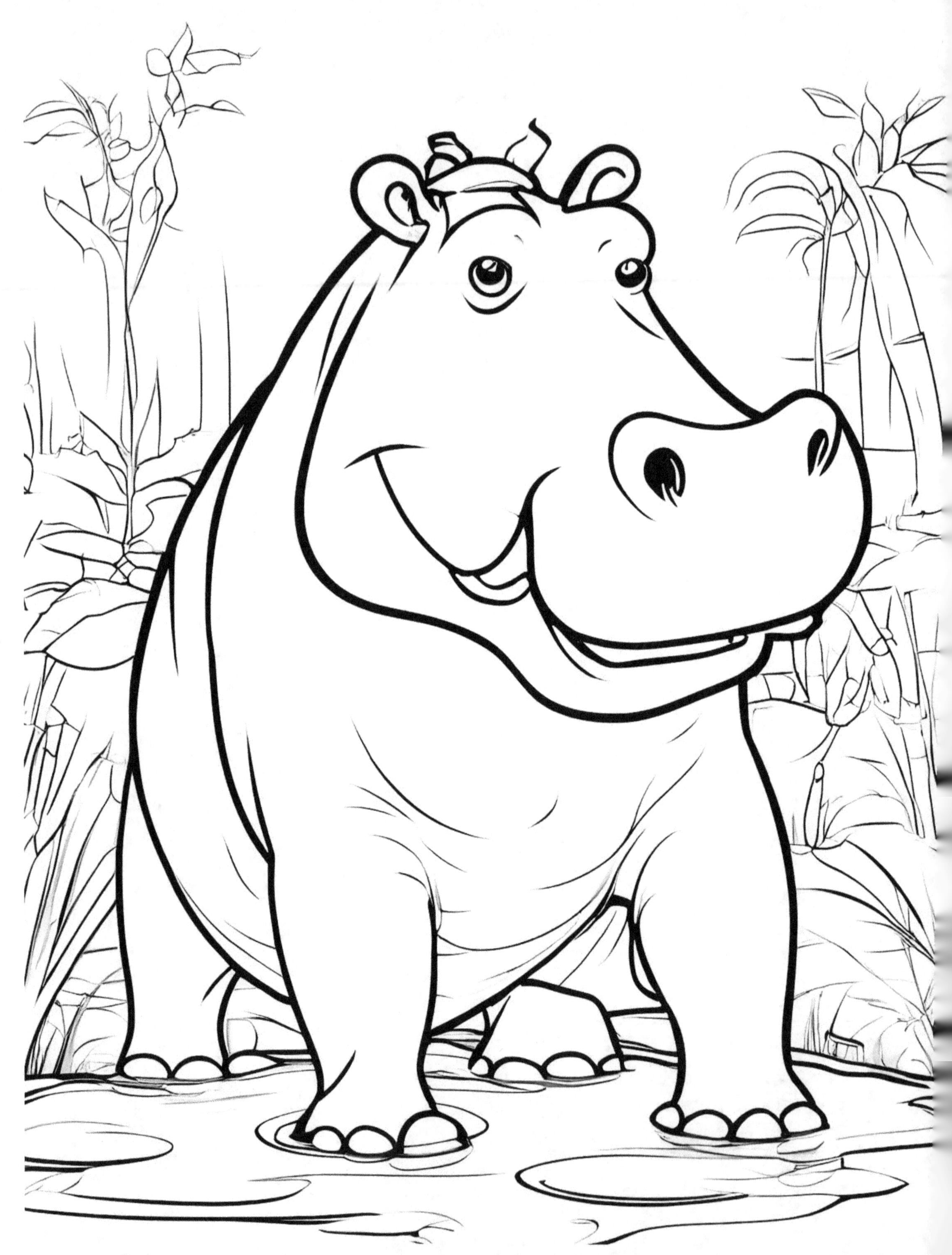

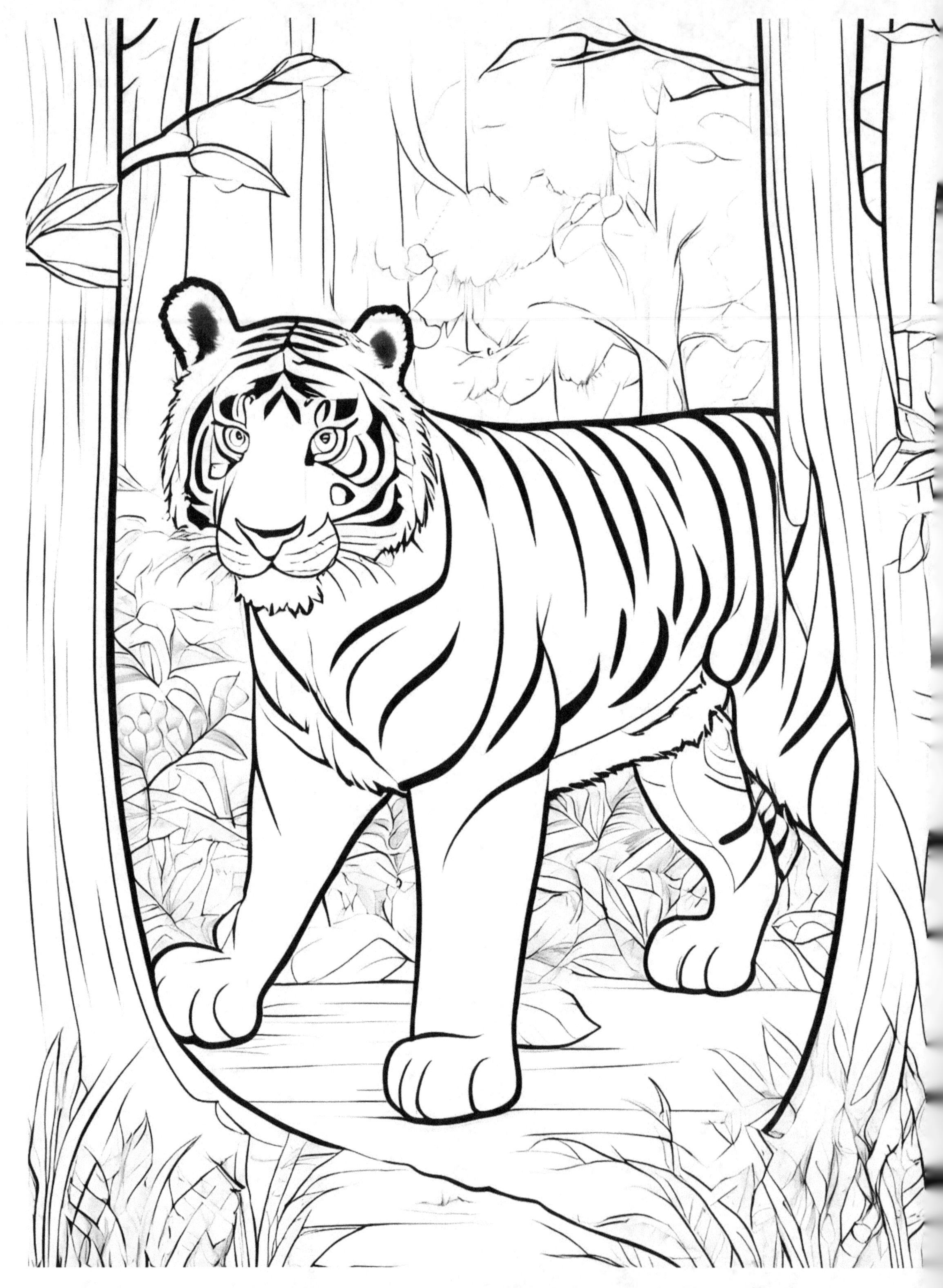

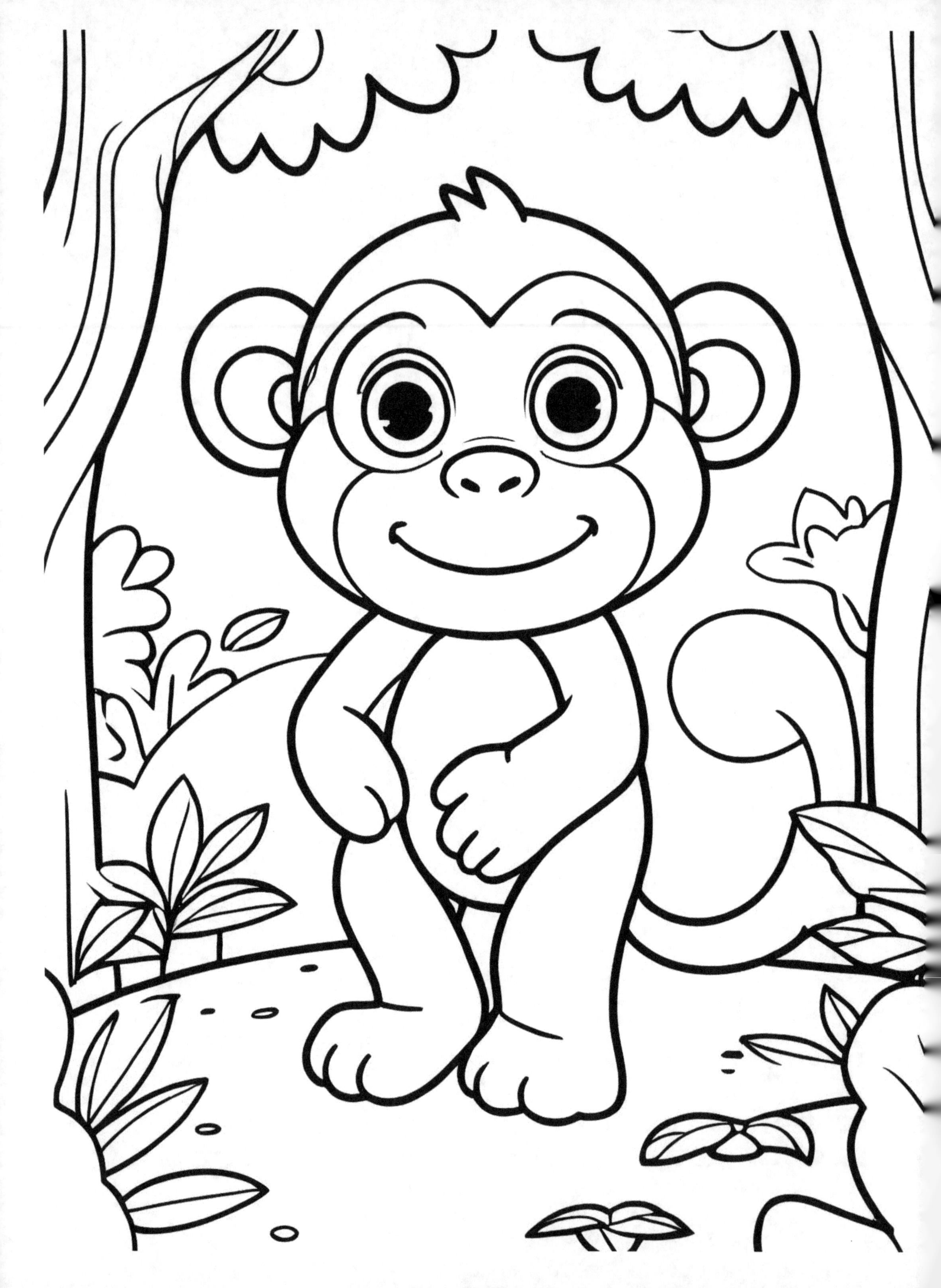

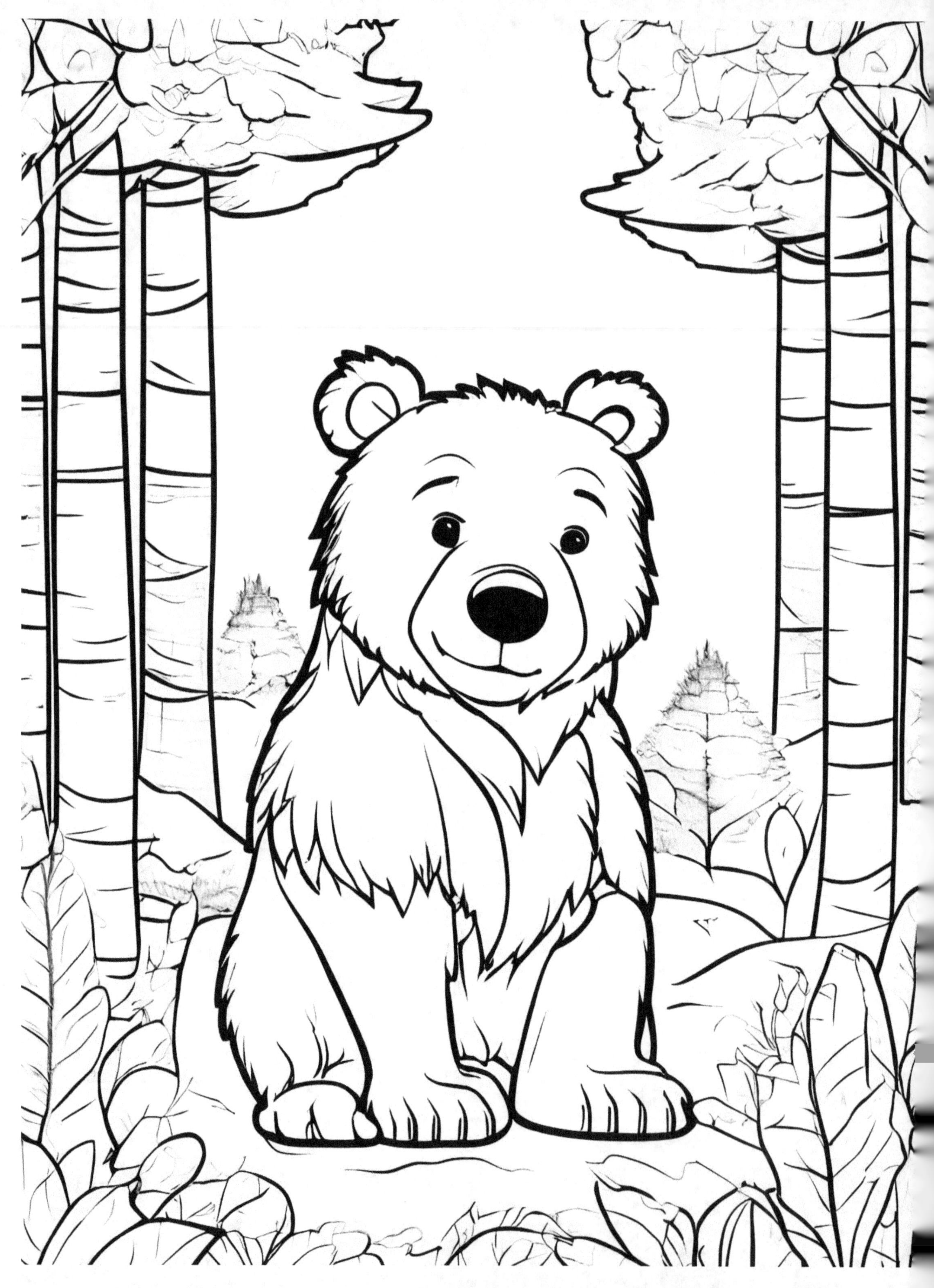

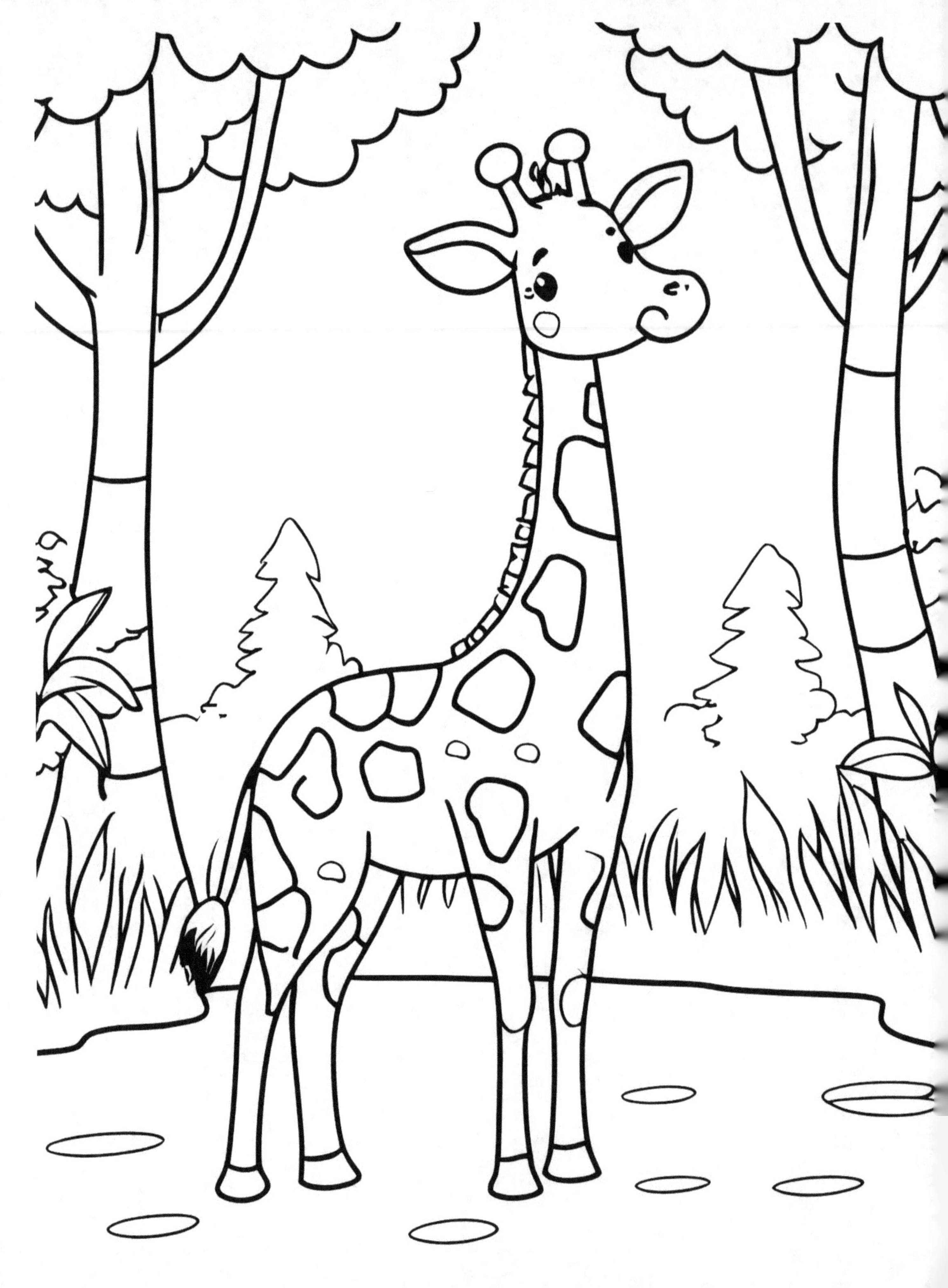

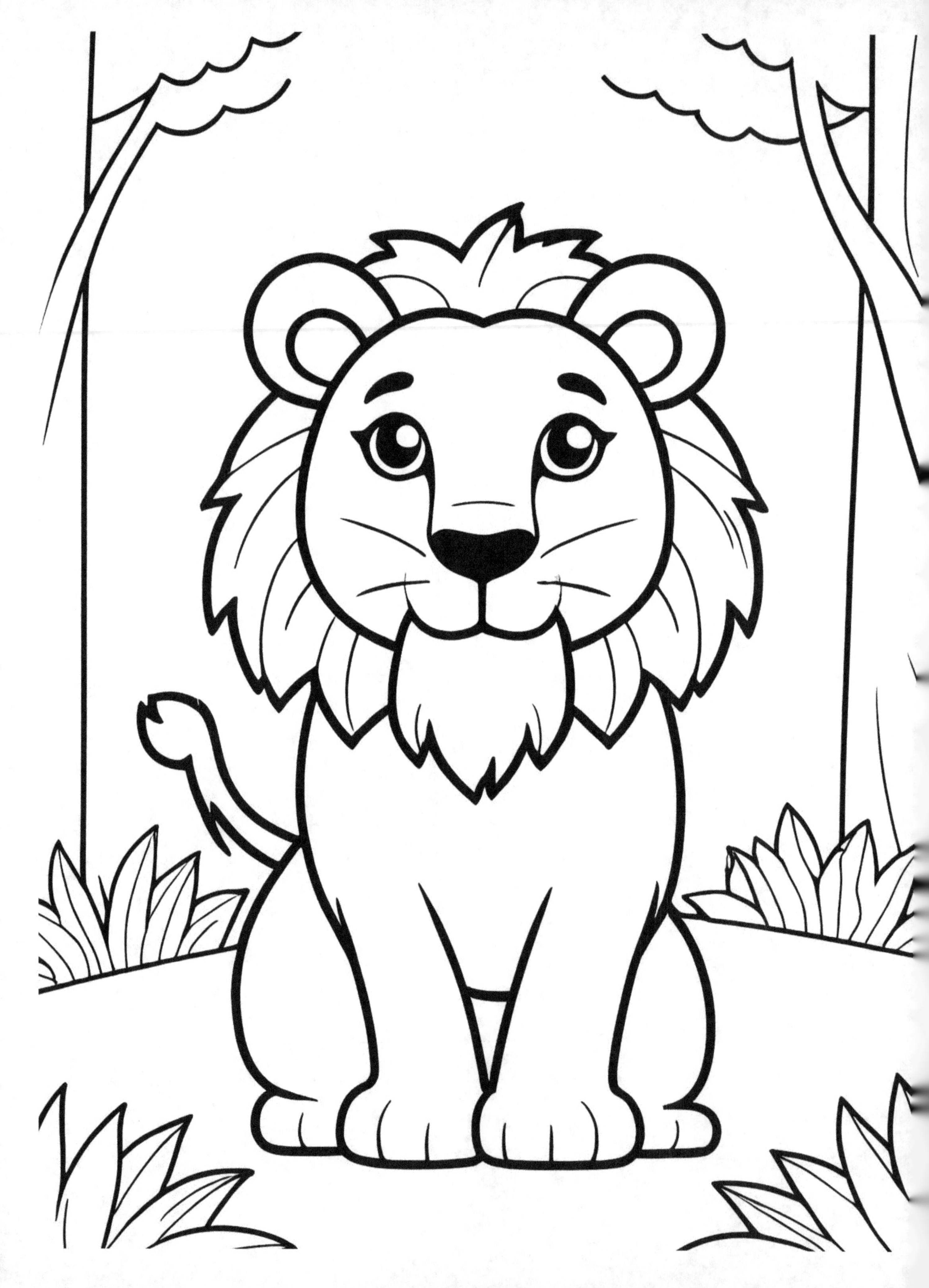

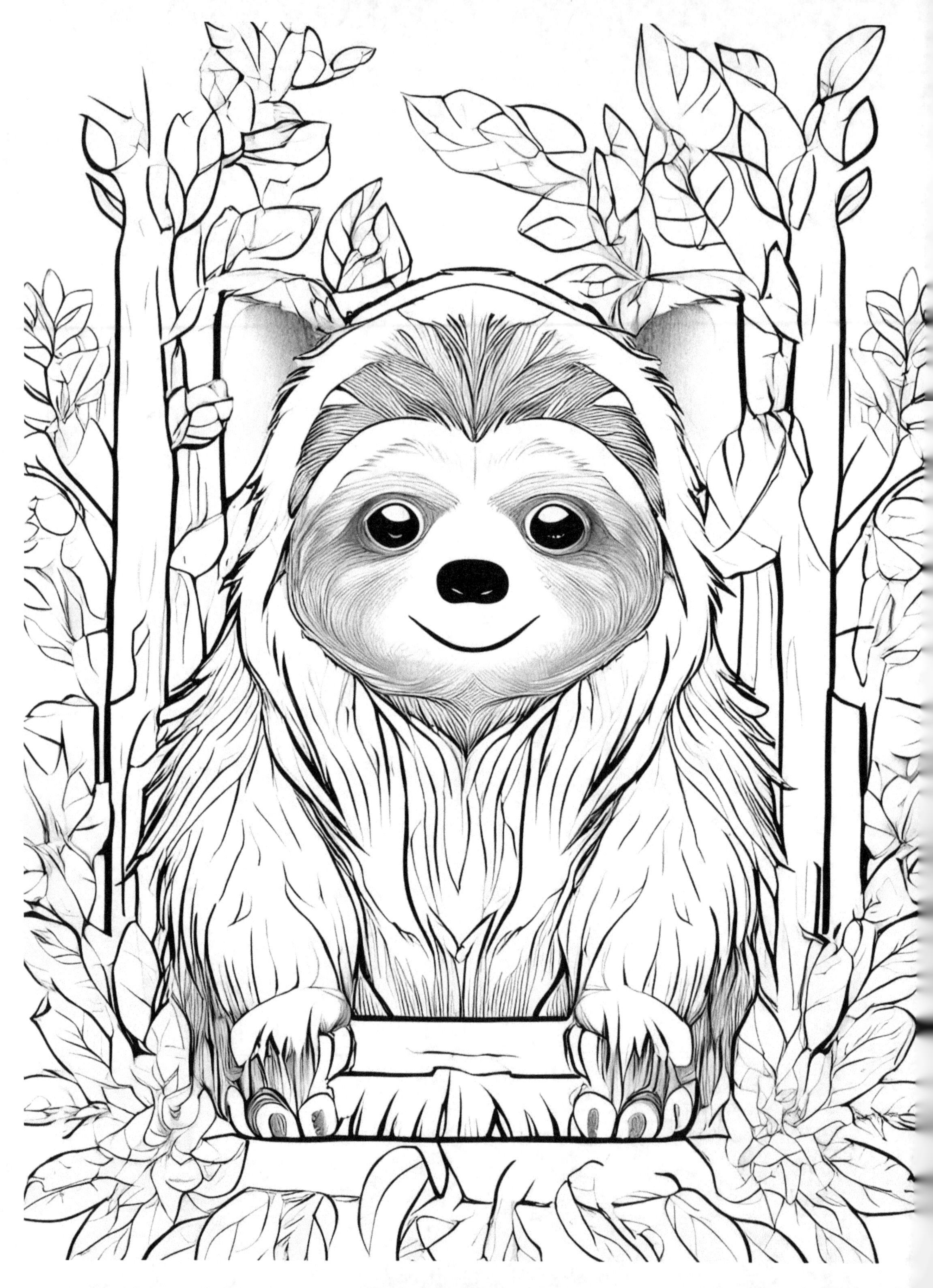

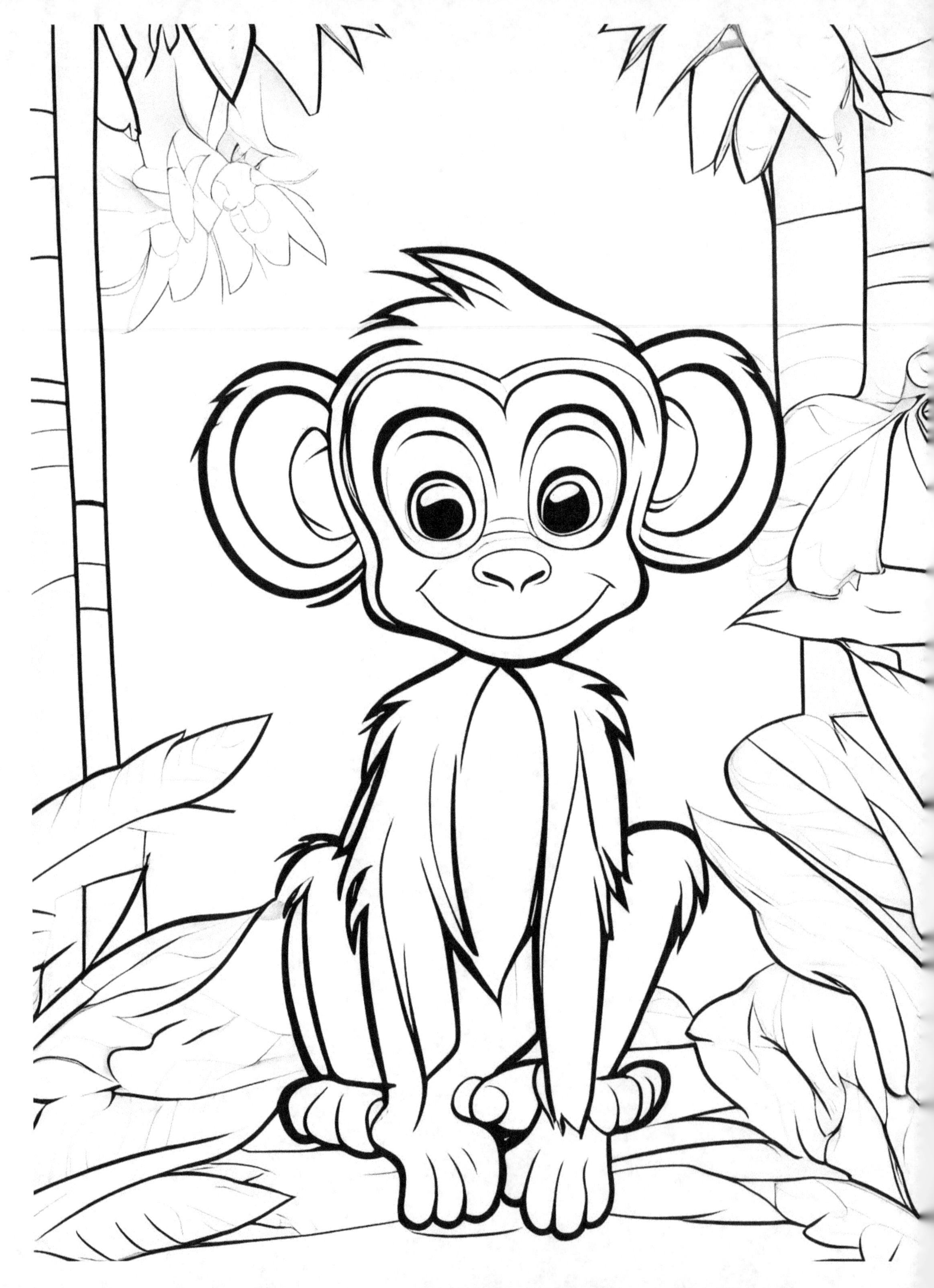

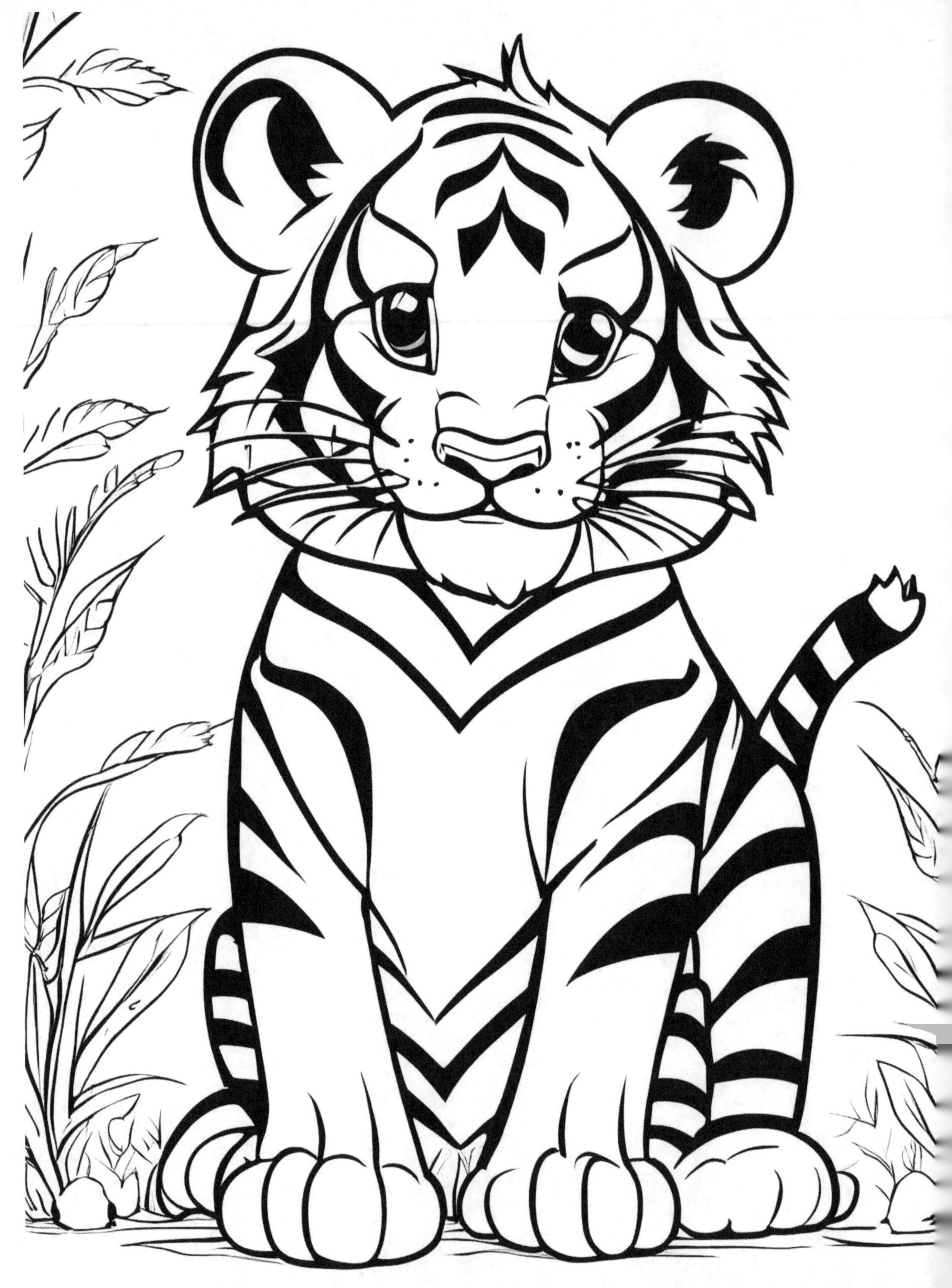

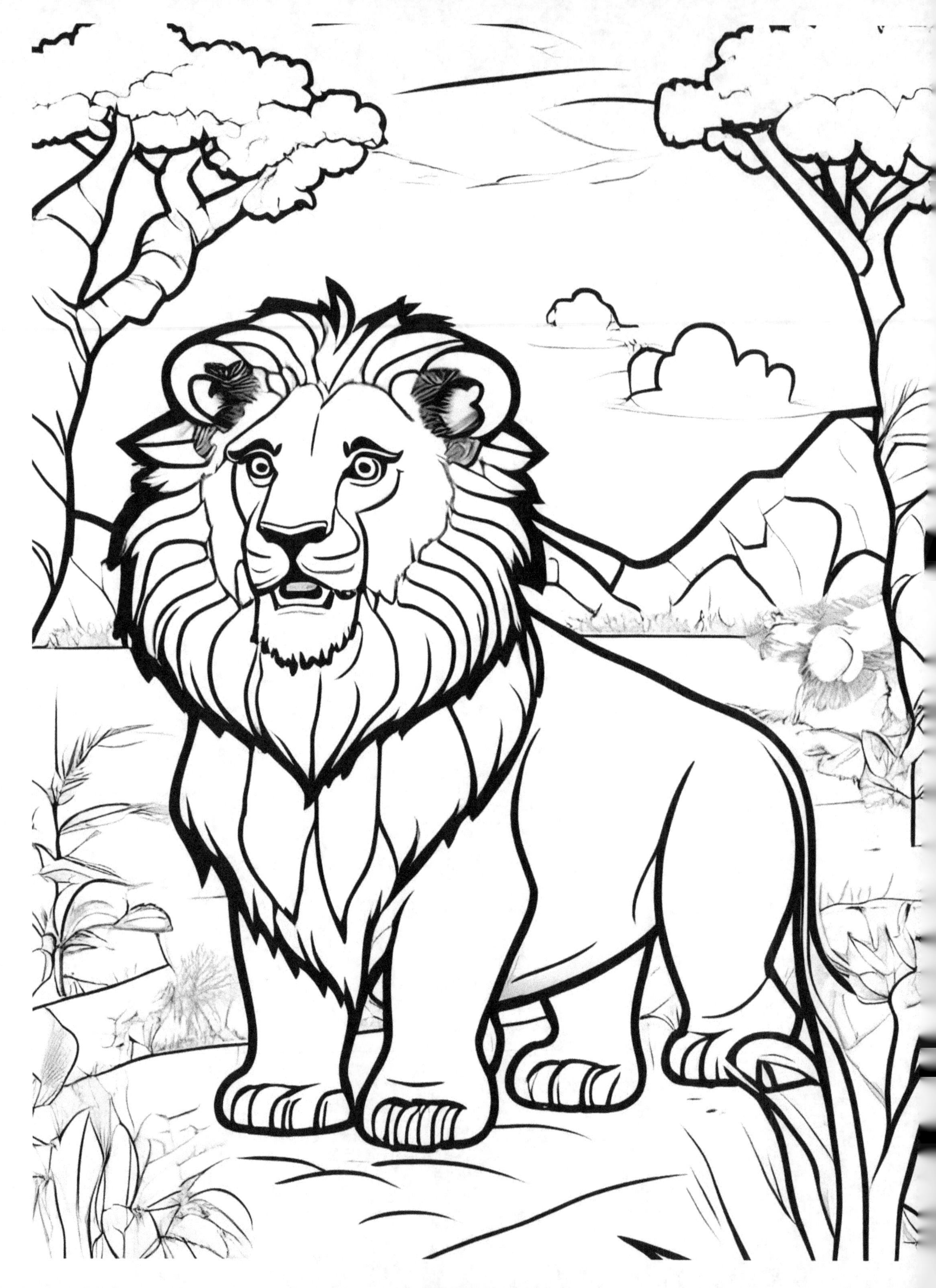

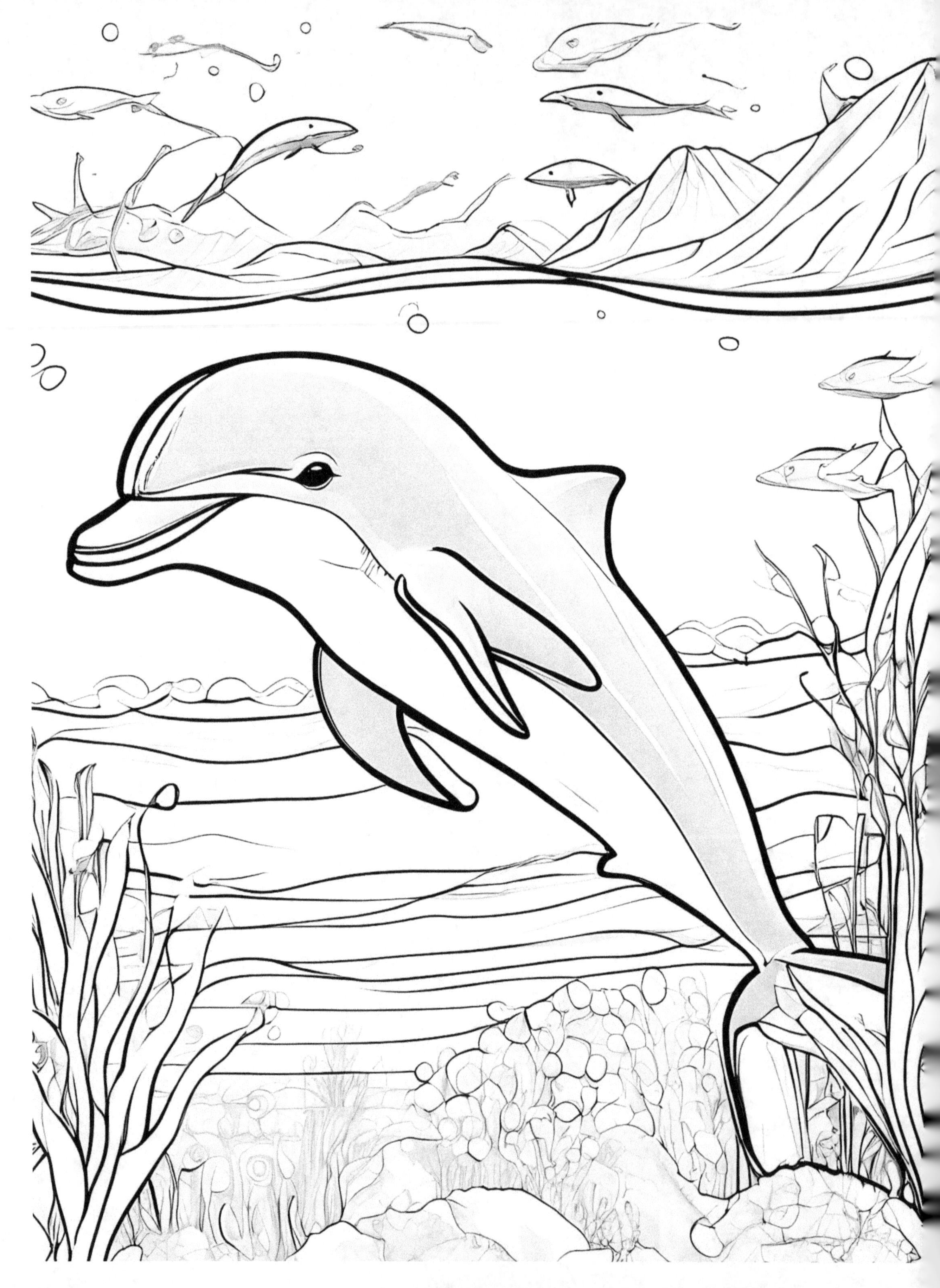

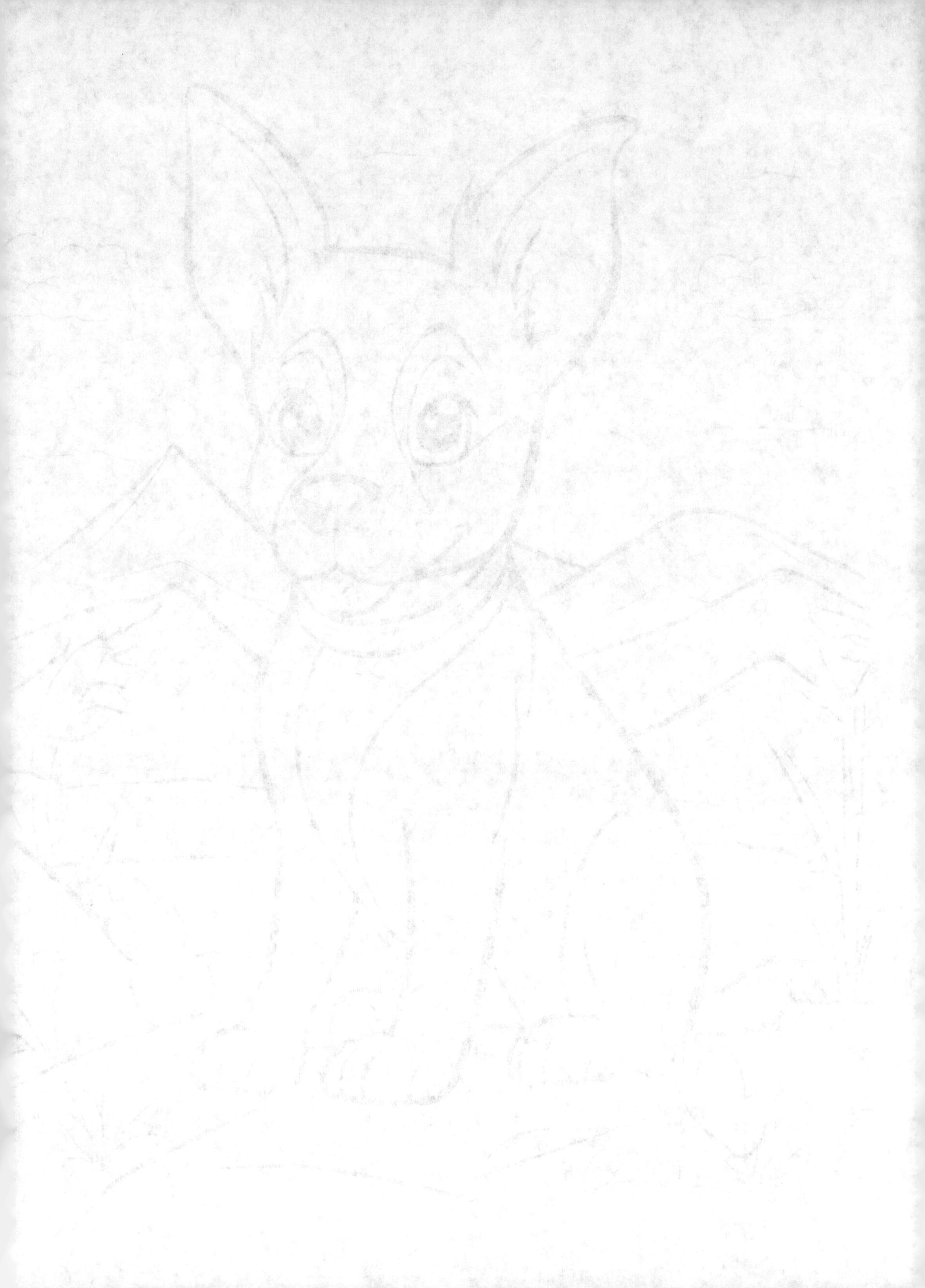

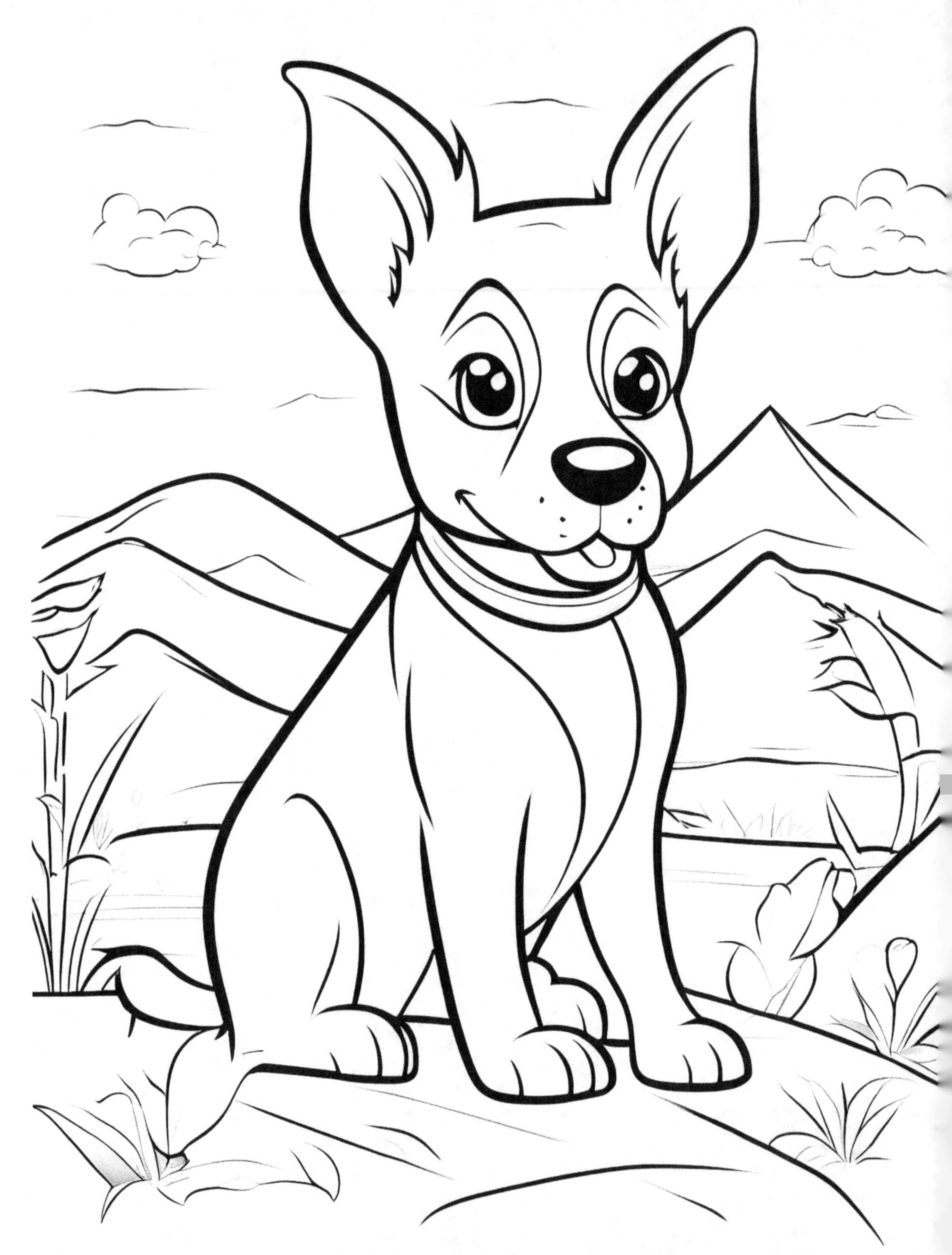

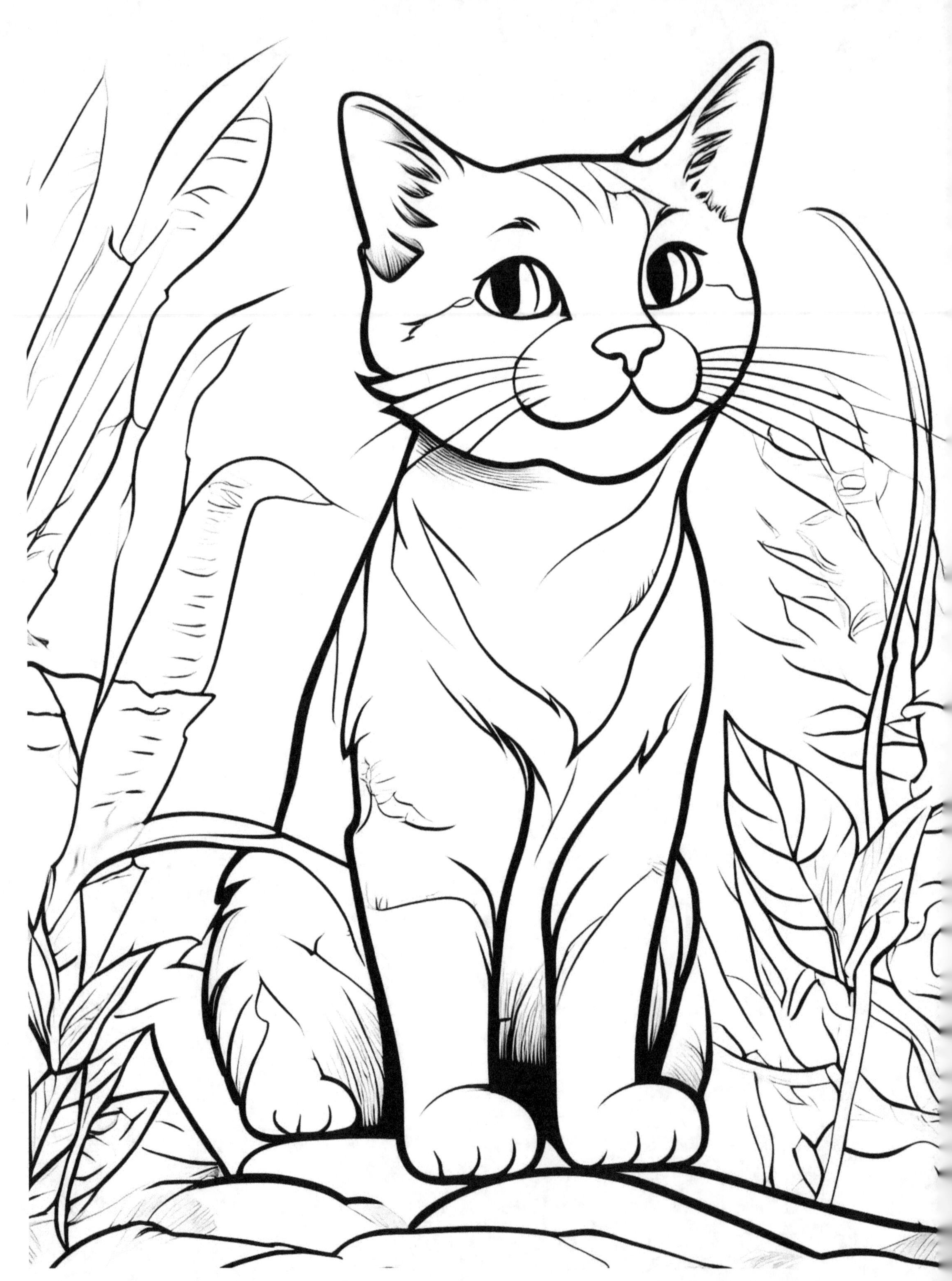

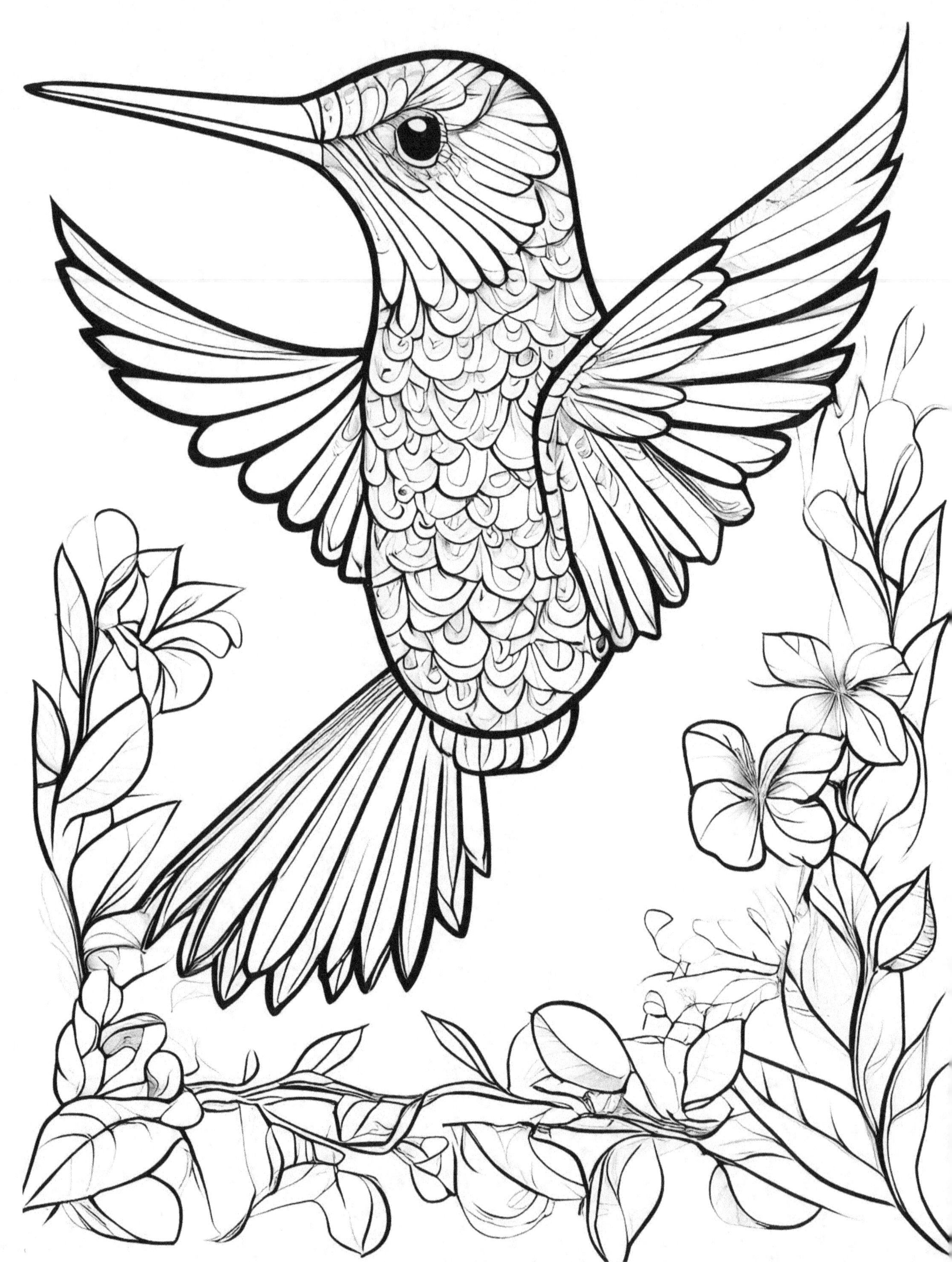